TO PETE,
THANKS FOR ALL
YOUR AWESOME
SUPPORT + FRIENDSHIP,
FOR MY SIS TOO!
I HOPE YOU
TAKE THIS TO
HEART.

BEST,

Matt

The Center Of The Universe
Is Right Between Your Eyes
But Home Is Where The Heart Is

By

Matthew J. Pallamary

Mystic Ink Publishing

Mystic Ink Publishing
San Diego, CA
www.mysticinkpublishing.com

© *2017 Matthew J. Pallamary. All Rights Reserved,*

ISBN 10: 0998680923 (sc)
ISBN 13: 978-0-9986809-2-7 (sc)

Library of Congress Control Number: 2017917220
Mystic Ink Publishing, San Diego, CA

Book Jacket and Page Design: Matthew J. Pallamary / San Diego CA
Cover artwork: William Llerena Murayari / Pucallpa Peru
Author's Photograph: Matthew J. Pallamary -- Gibbs Photo / Malibu CA

DEDICATION

This book is dedicated to Dr. Stanley Krippner Ph.D., friend, mentor, and a truly generous soul whose pioneering research laid much of the groundwork for this volume of my own studies and equally to Ken Symington whose invaluable guidance, friendship, and mentoring in my fieldwork filled in all the missing pieces.

Acknowledgements

The author would like to thank Rob and Kim Gubala whose support on so many levels made this book possible and to my sister Colleen Pallamary, proof reader extraordinaire.

.

TABLE OF CONTENTS

INTRODUCTION

Who or what are we really?

How do you define yourself?

Good? Evil? Sinner? Saint? Lover? Fighter? Christian? Muslim? Buddhist? Atheist?

Conservative? Liberal? Anarchist?

Executive? Artist? Lawyer? Musician? Firefighter? Cop?

Gay? Straight? Transgender? Polyamorous?

God's greatest gift or worthless and unworthy of being loved?

If you can quiet the chatter of your "monkey mind" long enough to examine your inner life with some objectivity, and pay close attention to what goes on there, you will become aware of how quickly it can change from instant to instant depending on what is happening in the moment (time) and the context (space).

In truth each of us are our own unique mercurial mixture of identities that we created from the center of our personal universe, and in each moment we may be motivated by emotion, intellect, or physical desire. More often than not, it is some shifting combination of the three.

When we are highly stimulated, agitated, or threatened in some way, this mass of competing energies whip up psychological gale force winds that can spin around inside and outside of us, often gathering strength to the point of eliciting physical, verbal, or emotional responses. Crimes of passion are an extreme example of this and in the aftermath we often hear denial in the words, "I don't know what got into me, I wasn't myself," or, "I blacked out."

That is the power that these primal energies hold, and we are the zero point nexus of their expression at the eye of the storm making us their gatekeeper if we are aware enough to take responsibility for who we are, how we think, and what we do. If we are swept up in the maelstrom to the point where we "lose our mind", then we disconnect like the proverbial leaf caught in the wind blown about by overwhelming forces that possess or take us over before we realize what is happening, sometimes with regrettable outcomes that we deny responsibility for.

This denial is an integral part of the reaction that comes in the aftermath of these impulses that project blame in the form of judgments onto who or what is considered the source of their provocation, yet the outburst originated from inside of the one acting out, making them the vehicle of its expression.

Here lies the contradiction, or better still, a paradox, which is a statement that despite apparently sound reasoning from true premises, leads to a self-contradictory or a logically unacceptable conclusion. A paradox involves contradictory yet interrelated elements that exist simultaneously and persist over time.

How do we overcome this impasse?

Many people attempt to assuage the discomfort of this contradiction by confessing to a priest, or by following a guru or some other spiritual leader or guide to "relieve them of the burden of their sins" and "find guidance on the path".

Unfortunately, this is another form of denial because by shedding our burden we are passing them off to our guru, guide, or confessor for absolution that robs us of personal responsibility for what *we* have manifested.

Self-proclaimed gurus are themselves more sophisticated purveyors of the lies of denial who claim to be enlightened, and are masters at drawing the lost and searching into their wake, which in effect pulls the searchers outside of themselves away from the source where their conflict originates, lulling them into a false sense of security. These "false prophets" consciously or subconsciously have a hidden agenda and suffer from what can be called guru-itis, which puts them in a false position of power and adoration from their followers, adding to an increasing self-perpetuating sense of self-delusional authority. The more unwarranted attention they get, the stronger their illusion of power becomes and the less they have to look at their own shortcomings. Their attention is focused outward and away from themselves, lavished upon their adoring flock.

By now it should be apparent that we are "ground zero", the focal point and origin of these psychological gale force winds that spin inside and outside of us. It should also be apparent that the process of our external projections no matter what form or forms they take, keep us outwardly directed, away from the source of their manifestation.

All that we deny about ourselves constitute what is known as our shadow, which in Jungian psychology refers to an unconscious aspect of our personality that the conscious ego does not identify in itself. In other words it is our "dark side". Because we tend to reject or remain ignorant of these least desirable aspects of our personalities, our shadow is largely negative and consists of everything that we are not fully conscious of.

There are, however, positive aspects that can remain hidden, especially in people with low self-esteem, anxieties, and false beliefs. To truly know ourselves we must accept our dark side and to deal with the dark side of others, we have to know our own.

Our shadow can include everything outside the light of consciousness, and may be positive or negative. "Everyone carries a shadow," Jung wrote, "and the less it is embodied in the individual's conscious life, the blacker and denser it is." It may be (in part) one's link to more primitive animal instincts, which are superseded during early childhood by the conscious mind.

According to Jung, the shadow, in being instinctive and irrational, is prone to psychological projection, in which a perceived personal inferiority is recognized as a perceived moral deficiency in someone else. Jung writes that if these projections remain hidden, "The projection-making factor (the Shadow archetype) then has a free hand and can realize its object--if it has one--or bring about some other situation characteristic of its power." These projections insulate and harm individuals by acting as a constantly thickening veil of illusion between the ego and the real world.

Jung also believed that "in spite of its function as a reservoir for human darkness—or perhaps because of this—the shadow is the seat of creativity"; so that for some, it may be, "the dark side of his being, his sinister shadow...represents the true spirit of life as against the arid scholar."

In those moments when we get disconnected by getting emotionally mugged and project outward by forces that are out of our control, what if we looked *into* the darkness and did a pre-emptive disconnect ahead of the unexpected hurricane that sweeps us away like so many leaves in the wind?

What if we took full responsibility for who and what we are and became our own gurus, brave enough to venture into what we mortally fear down to the core of our very being?

What treasures might lie buried in the blackness of that terrifying abyss waiting to reward those courageous enough to confront the dragons and demons that guard it?

Regardless of the direction we take, we exist in the center of a choice between conscious responsible action that influences our thoughts, beliefs, and actions both inside and outside of us, or we can surrender and be victims to fear based programmed re-actions.

This ground zero choice point has the potential to provide a glimpse into the concept that the center of the universe is right between your eyes. Read on if you want to explore the possibilities of freeing your spirit and reclaiming your inheritance as the creator you were meant to be.

SUBJECTIVITY -- A STUDY IN PERCEPTION

No matter how you choose to define yourself, in the end you and you alone are the one who does the defining. If you define yourself according to the judgment and expectations of others, you have lost yourself to a no-win situation, because no matter what you do, it is impossible to please everyone; yet with so many voices, thoughts, and impulses competing for your time, attention, and energy, how do you find a balance that brings peace?

Where is the center?

The true center where inner peace can be found lies in the "eye of the storm" that everything in your inner and outer life revolves around and this can only be found by practicing conscious awareness, which is an act of personal will. By paying attention and doing the challenging work that is constantly under assault and derailed by the spinning maelstrom of the monkey mind that is the ego, or more accurately egos that make up our inner lives, we have the ability to unify these disparate energies that spin through us with their own agendas.

All of this happens in our minds where we interpret and define our experience of reality at the choice point where we reside between objectivity and subjectivity. If we focus on paying attention we will develop what can be called witness consciousness and discover the meaning of the expression, "Where your attention goes, there your energy goes."

If cultivated, witness consciousness becomes the self-created focal point produced by harnessing the energy of awareness that takes responsibility for all of our thoughts and actions by paying attention and simply observing.

The Zen concept of non-attachment provides a good example of what witness consciousness entails, which is characterized as a practice of presence and mindfulness, while not allowing our sense of well being to rely upon anything other than our own presence of awareness. It means to be in the world, but not of the world.

This is different from detachment, which is distancing ourselves from the world out of disinterest with an aloofness that separates us from the rest of the world, resulting in escapism, another form of suffering.

Non-attachment means that our happiness is no longer defined by anything outside of us. It is selfless because our sense of 'self' is no longer inserted into every situation. We are no longer self-centered and we can become single-pointed in our awareness of other people. If we allow our sense of self to be emotionally swayed by everything that appears to us, including people, places, perceptions, thoughts, sensations, events, experiences, and all seeming things, then our emotions will forever be taking us on a roller-coaster of ups and downs, swinging between joy and disaster. Our sense of well being will always be based on what we allow ourselves to be emotionally attached to, and when we become attached to something our happiness is based on a shifting duality that defines us by the outside world, rather than our true inner nature.

Witness consciousness represents freedom that comes from a self-realization of the truth, that you, the consciousness that resides at the center of the universe that you are taking charge of and responsibility for, cannot be affected by anything. It is only the egoic mind(s) that make you believe otherwise.

G.I Gurdjieff, an influential mystic and spiritual leader of the early twentieth century characterized witness consciousness in one of his lectures.

"Instead of the discordant and often contradictory activity of different desires, there is *one single I*, whole, indivisible, and permanent; there is individuality, dominating the physical body and its desires and able to overcome both its reluctance and its resistance. Instead of the mechanical process of thinking there is *consciousness*. And there is *will*, that is, a power, not merely composed of various often contradictory desires belonging to different 'I's', but issuing from consciousness and governed by

individuality or a single and permanent I. Only such a will can be called 'free', for it is independent of accident and cannot be altered or directed from without."

Our five primary mechanisms of perception come from our sense receptors; taste, sight, touch, smell, and hearing. With the exception of our sense of touch, which comes to us through all parts of our bodies, our other four senses come through our head, which filters and puts them together into the unique perspective that we as individuals harbor whether we define the world through "rose colored glasses" or the dingy windows of a depressed outlook.

Aside from the subject/object ground zero that puts the center of our universe between our eyes where we decide what our reality consists of according to our interpretation of these impressions, this location is the most logical place to locate it based on the construction of our body and the way our senses are arrayed about our head.

This focus of awareness whether physical, mental, or metaphysical, points to the notion of the third eye, also called the mind's eye or inner eye that represents a mystical and esoteric concept that refers to a speculative invisible eye reputed to provide perception beyond ordinary sight.

This third eye is considered to be the extension of what the mind perceives in the form of a subconscious awareness of the surroundings and interactions of the environment. In some spiritual traditions the third eye refers to the gate that leads to inner realms and spaces of higher consciousness, and in our present "new age" spirituality it often symbolizes a state of enlightenment or the evocation of mental images having deep personal, spiritual, or psychological significance. Some Christian teachings view the concept of the third eye as a metaphor for non-dualistic thinking; the way the mystics see.

The rudiments of a biological basis for the mind's eye is found in the deeper portions of the brain below the neocortex *where the center of perception exists.* The neocortex is characterized as a sophisticated memory storage warehouse where data received as an input from sensory systems is compartmentalized via the cerebral cortex which allows shapes to be identified. Given the lack of filtering input produced internally, we have the ability to hallucinate and see things that aren't received as external input, but as internal. Not all people have the same internal perceptual ability. For many, when their eyes

15

are closed, the perception of darkness prevails, however some people are able to perceive colorful, dynamic imagery.

In Theosophy the third eye is typically related to the pineal gland. According to this theory, humans had in far ancient times an actual third eye in the back of the head with a physical and spiritual function. Over time, as humans evolved, this eye atrophied and sank into what today is known as the pineal gland.

Dr. Rick Strassman has hypothesized that the pineal gland, which maintains light sensitivity, is responsible for the production and release of DMT (dimethyltryptamine), an entheogen which he believes could be excreted in large quantities at the moments of birth and death.

The pineal gland is a small endocrine gland in the vertebrate brain with a shape that resembles a pine cone, hence its name. It is located near the center of the brain, between the two hemispheres, tucked in a groove where the two halves of the thalamus join. From the point of view of biological evolution, the pineal gland represents a kind of atrophied photoreceptor, and in the epithalamus of some species of amphibians and reptiles it is linked to a light-sensing organ known as the parietal eye, which is also called the pineal eye or *third eye*. Philosopher René Descartes believed the pineal gland to be the "principal seat of the soul".

Phenomenology is the Western philosophical tradition that has most forcefully called into question the modern assumption of a single, wholly determinable, objective reality and it has its source in Descartes' well-known separation of the thinking mind or subject, from the material world of things, or objects. This philosophy formed the basis for the divide-and-conquer western scientific method which has shown us many things, but ultimately falls short in comprehending the vastness of reality the way that shamans who are in touch with the natural world do. Instead of showing us more, our divide and conquer mentality has largely resulted in isolating us by technology and civilization in a divide that has grown by greater and greater degrees in modern times.

In terms of this growing separation, French phenomenologist Maurice Merleau-Ponty stated:

"All my knowledge of the world, even my scientific knowledge, is gained from my own particular point of view, or from some experience of the world without which the symbols of science would be meaningless. The whole universe of science is built upon the world as directly experienced, and if we want to subject science itself to rigorous scrutiny and arrive at a precise assessment of its meaning and scope, we must begin by reawakening the basic experience of the world, of which science is the second - order expression... To return to things themselves is to return to that world which precedes knowledge, of which knowledge always *speaks*, and in relation to which every scientific schematization is an abstract and derivative sign-language, as is geography in relation to the countryside in which we have learnt beforehand what a forest, a prairie or a river is."

Regardless of our conception of the third eye or the mind's eye, whether physical, mental, or metaphysical, we cannot disregard the fact that the primary focus of our awareness and the creation of reality as we know it lies in our subjective interpretation of a world that exists through us and around us.

Aside from these physical, mental, and subjective indicators of the location Descartes refers to as the seat of the soul, for the more scientific minded among us there are objective indicators evident in physics, the branch of science concerned with the nature and properties of matter and energy that includes mechanics, heat, light and other radiation, sound, electricity, magnetism, and the structure of atoms.

This phenomenon is known as the observer effect, which is the fact that simply observing a situation necessarily changes it. Physicists have discovered that even passive observation of quantum phenomena can in fact change it.

No matter how you characterize the subject object paradox, the fact of the matter is that in the end it comes down to a matter of perception; something that brings us all back to our primordial roots.

Who better to teach us about the nature of perception than the ancient masters of perception themselves, shamans, who train to master extreme altered states of consciousness that makes them masters of a flexible perspective that gives them the ability to navigate multidimensional realms and energies that the uninitiated can scarcely imagine.

THE WORLD'S OLDEST PROFESSION

The World's Oldest Profession is not what we have been told by popular culture. The *real* world's oldest profession is shamanism, which is an amalgam of the world's oldest professions with roots that range well beyond our historical stereotypes of witch doctors, wild men, and demonically possessed primitives. Among other things, shamans were the first doctors, performing artists, musicians, storytellers, teachers, priests, psychologists, and magicians, who performed critical functions in their societies.

Magicians, whether modern entertainers or indigenous tribal sorcerers work with the malleable texture of perception.
Ecologist, philosopher, and sleight-of-hand magician David Abram, Ph.D., tells us in his brilliant work on language and perception titled, *The Spell of the Sensuous*:

"In tribal cultures that which we call "magic" takes its meaning from the fact that humans, and in indigenous and oral context, experience their own consciousness as simply one form of awareness among many others. The traditional magician cultivates an ability to shift out of his or her common state of consciousness precisely in order to make contact with the other organic forms of sensitivity and awareness with which human existence is entwined. Only by temporarily shedding the accepted perceptual logic of his culture can the sorcerer hope to enter into relation with other species on their own terms; only by altering the common organization of his senses will he be able to

enter into a rapport with the multiple nonhuman sensibilities that animate the local landscape. It is this, we might say, that defines a shaman: the ability to readily slip out of the perceptual boundaries that demarcate his or her particular culture -- boundaries reinforced by social customs, taboos, and most importantly, the common speech or language -- in order to make contact with, and learn from, the other powers in the land. His magic is precisely this heightened receptivity to the meaningful solicitations -- songs, cries, gestures -- of the larger, more than human field.

Magic, then, and it's perhaps most primordial sense, is the experience of existing in the world made up of multiple intelligences, the intuition that every form one perceives -- from the swallow swooping overhead to the fly on a blade of grass, and indeed the blade of grass itself -- is an *experiencing* form, an entity with its own predilections and sensations, albeit sensations that are very different from our own."

The magic of shamanism constitutes a prehistoric belief system that not only carries the same traditions and practices across cultures worldwide, it also continues to infuse our world with deeper meaning. Shamans were the first medical specialists in indigenous communities whose traditional methods have been effective in treating both physical and psychological ailments. The chemical components of plants used in shamanic healing rites have the potential to be building blocks for new drugs or cures for such scourges as cancer, heart disease, diabetes, Alzheimer's, and many others.

The World Health Organization estimates that 80 percent of the people in developing countries still rely on traditional medicine for their primary health care needs. Without money, access, or faith in modern facilities, indigenous people depend on shamans and herbal healers for their survival. Shamans also play a crucial role in helping scientists to discover the potentials of plants. As one scientist has said, "Each time a medicine man dies, it is as if a library has been burned down."

When asked about the roots of his tradition, and aging jungle healer stated, "I am a plant man. My father was a plant man as was his father before him and his father before him as far back as can be remembered."

This simple statement is living testimony to prehistoric wisdom still being passed on through myths, practices, and belief systems kept alive through oral traditions the way they have for thousands of years from a distant past with roots that extend well beyond anything conceivable in our present "information age", and in many respects far removed from it.

There is added depth to the uses of plants and other healing knowledge carried in the cultural collective that can only be accessed through direct subjective experience learned in visionary states engendered in a multitude of ways aside from or in combination with entheogenic plants, among them fasting, dancing, extreme diets, vision quests, ordeals, and many other time tested methods known to alter consciousness.

In the Peruvian Amazon and throughout much of South America, the primary shamanic healing practice is centered around the Ayahuasca Vine, referred to as the "Mother of the Plants". In these traditions, "Mother Ayahuasca" works with a multitude of other teacher plants, each with their own unique healing properties in special diets and treatments referred to as *dietas*.

Though it is the name of the actual vine, Ayahuasca refers to an entheogenic brew made out of the Ayahuasca vine known as *Banisteriopsis caapi*, and the *Psychotria viridis* leaf, referred to as Chacruna, a dimethyltryptamine (DMT)-containing plant species.

In the Quechua languages, *aya* means "spirit, soul, corpse, dead body", and *waska* means "rope" and "woody vine", or "liana". The word *Ayahuasca* has been variously translated as "liana of the soul", "liana of the dead", and "spirit liana".

This brew made from the two plants is taken in a ceremonial setting where it induces healing, cleansing, and purging as well as intense visionary states that communicate information in nonrational ways through alien feeling symbols, concepts, emotions, thoughts, vistas, and other mixed perceptions. Dense information unfolds through rapidly transforming geometric colors and patterns, often in the form of synesthesia, where perceptions cross. While all of the senses are heightened and transformed in inexplicable ways, what stands out in these altered states is that sound can be seen, color can be heard, and feeling can come in hues and colors that defy description.

Much of the traditional music of the Peruvian Amazon plays an integral part in Ayahuasca ceremonies. Songs are sung and music is performed as offerings to honor, flatter, and serenade the Mother, showing respect, as well as the healing and helping spirits of other plants and animal allies working with her so they will gift the petitioner with power, healing, wisdom, or other special gifts. In jungle lore, Mother Ayahuasca is the river that you journey upon and the sacred songs known as *icaros* are the boats that carry you on that journey. The multi-sensorial, multi-dimensional Ayahuasca journey is something that can never be fully articulated in any medium and can only truly be known through direct experience.

By gaining experiential knowledge given to them by the plants and the patterns of Mother Nature herself, shamans understand on an intuitive level that nature's designs are energy flows. Since prehistoric times, they have learned how the matrices of nature work together and with this knowledge they live in accord with these forces by embodying a balance of power that puts them in harmony with the forces of nature instead of in opposition to them the way we are in today's world.

Aside from being a bridge between the worlds, the path of the shaman is to become a man or woman of power and the way to accomplish that is to learn how to master energy in all of its manifestations and dimensions. Learning how to master the energies of altered states puts the shaman in a multitude of unpredictable and inexplicable subjective experiences that alter their perception of reality by changing their experience in the same way that a radio receiver changes the station it is receiving by tuning in to a different carrier frequency. By continually "changing stations" and assimilating different realms and experiences, including plant and animal realms, the shaman breaks the station lock of consensual reality which brings them a greater flexibility of perception that frees their perspective from the narrow way most people experience the world.

This is especially true in indigenous groups who by breaking the perceptual lock that most of us live in give equal weight and validity to waking, dreaming, and visions, so that they all cross over each other into one big palette of experience. This freeing of perception brings the magic and flexibility of the non-physical realities of dreaming and visions into the present moment of their "waking world" of consensual reality, rewarding them with an expanded awareness and fuller presence in whatever transitory moment they happen to be experiencing at any given instant, regardless of the energies or realities they may be tuned in to.

In spite of its seeming solidity and permanence, the physical waking world of consensual reality that we all share is in fact transitory. This inarguable point is driven home by the inevitability of our impending death.

EVERYTHING IS ENERGY
AND THAT'S ALL THERE IS TO IT

The genius inventor Nikola Tesla is quoted as saying, "If you want to find the secrets of the universe, think in terms of energy, frequency, and vibration.", which is something shamans have known intuitively since time immemorial.

Another quotation often attributed to Albert Einstein, is widely believed to come from a channeler who assigned the words to an entity named Bashar, who stated, "Everything is energy and that's all there is to it. Match the frequency of the reality you want and you cannot help but get that reality. It can be no other way. This is not philosophy. This is physics."

Einstein did speak about the relationship between matter and energy in a 1948 film called "Atomic Physics", where he stated, *"It followed from the special theory of relativity that mass and energy are both but different manifestations of the same thing — a somewhat unfamiliar conception for the average mind."*

Many years earlier, Gurdjieff stated the same concept in his own way.

"In the Absolute, or all is one, matter and force are also one. But in this connection matter and force are not taken as real principles of the world in itself, but as properties or characteristics of the phenomenal world observed by us. To begin the study of the universe it is sufficient to have an elementary idea of matter and energy, such as we get by immediate observation through our organs of sense. The

23

'constant' is taken as material, as matter, and 'changes' in the state of the 'constant', or of matter, are called manifestations of force or energy. All these changes can be regarded as the result of vibrations or undulatory motions which begin in center, that is, in the Absolute, and go in all directions, crossing one another, colliding, and merging together, until they stop all together at the end of the ray of creation."

"From this point of view, then, the world consists of vibrations and matter, or of matter in a state of vibration, a vibrating matter. The rate of vibration is in inverse ratio to the density of matter."

In other words, according to Tesla, Einstein, and Gurdjieff, three individuals considered to be geniuses of the twentieth century, everything *is* energy, and in the world view of a shaman *everything* without question is energy whether it be waking reality, dreams, visions, solid objects, emotions, sights, sounds, smells, or any other sensations. Indigenous shamans do not separate dreaming, waking, or visionary worlds. To them it is all one continuum, and each realm carries just as much weight and validity as the other, and all of them are connected in one interactive whole. Modern day quantum physicists have also embraced this as a result of two principles they have learned through the close scientific observation of energetic principles in action.

The first is non-locality or action at a distance, which refers to the direct interaction of two objects that are separated in space with no perceivable intermediate agency or mechanism. The second principle is quantum non-locality which refers to what Einstein called the "spooky action at a distance" of quantum entanglement, a physical phenomenon that occurs when pairs or groups of particles are generated or interact in ways where the quantum state of each particle cannot be described independently. Instead, a quantum state is given for the system as a whole, which proves that everything is connected to everything else, whether seen or unseen.

The second principle is that of a hologram which we know of as an image composed of a great number of small parts, all of which contain the image as a whole. When a hologram is broken into many pieces, what remains is many small but complete images of the whole.

The ocean provides another example of what constitutes a holographic reality.

Since it is made up of water, we can say that the ocean is contained in every drop. Similarly, a ray of the Sun contains the Sun itself, and in a seed, the entire structure of the tree is contained within it. Additionally, every cell of our body contains the complete information about the entire mind-body system. Each of the 100 billion cells that make up our bodies contain the complete version of the original DNA which was the source of the entire body.

All levels of creation are analogous to each other because each level of creation is an expression of the whole, interpreted through a different vibratory lens that constitutes a unique perspective, and every single thing within this interconnected reality is made of energy. For a shaman to become a master of reality they must follow what is called the power path which amounts to becoming a master of energy.

The word *energy* is derived from the Ancient Greek expression: ἐνέργεια *energeia* "activity, operation", which is believed to appear for the first time in the work of Aristotle. In contrast to the modern definition, energeia was a qualitative philosophical concept broad enough to include ideas such as happiness and pleasure. Every emotion that we feel, we experience as a different kind of energy, and each has its own unique qualities.

In physics, energy is a property of objects, transferable among them via fundamental interactions, which can be converted in form, but not created or destroyed. Energy transformation or energy conversion is the process of changing one form of energy to another which is what happens to shamans in their journey to the underworld where they are dismembered and reborn anew by facing their deepest fears.

Energy indicates movement and movement denotes the process of transformation. If you start with the simplest geometric concept of a point, it is a coordinate that has no dimension, and it is static and unmoving. If you extend that point in one direction, you have a line. The more energy that is put out to overcome inertia, the further that point moves and the longer the line becomes, so a longer line is a sign of more expended energy.

The distance between these two points contain the potential, which in the study of electricity is called voltage, electrical potential difference, electric tension or electric pressure -- the electric potential difference between two points, or the difference in electric potential energy of a unit charge transported between two points.

Implicit in the difference between two points is the concept of polarity which is denoted by two poles labeled positive and negative. Batteries, fuel cells and solar cells all produce this **direct current, known as DC.** The terminals of a battery are always, respectively, positive and negative and current always flows in the same direction between those two terminals.

The power that comes from a power plant on the other hand is **alternating current, known as AC** where the direction of the current reverses or alternates 60 times per second in the U.S. or 50 times per second in Europe.

There are two characteristic of alternating current that come into play with this concept of movement which are known as amplitude and frequency.

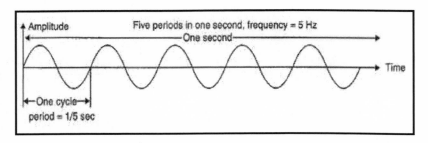

The greater the amplitude of a wave, the higher the level of energy that it carries. With a sound wave, this means that the sound will be louder. With light, the bigger amplitude means the light will be brighter. In water, the bigger the amplitude of the waves, the higher they will be. Frequency is the number of occurrences of a repeating event per unit time, so the higher the frequency, the more there is happening in each moment.

All of these characteristics of energy fall under the laws of physics, a natural science that involves the study of matter and its motion through space-time and its related concepts of energy and force. More broadly, it is the general analysis of nature, conducted in order to understand how the universe behaves.

In order to navigate the physical world our senses take in a multitude of stimuli, much of it through the eyes and ears. What our senses take in, our minds process continuously, reinterpreting the incoming data from moment to moment, instantaneously making adjustments to the shifting environment. By regulating our breathing, heartbeat, and blood pressure, as well as other unconscious physiological functions, our body's natural intelligence strives for balance; especially when it is involved in intense physical activity that requires great coordination, like sports or dancing.

This rapid exchange between inner subjectivity and outer objectivity is an infinity pattern between external stimulus and inner interpretation. The continuous volley and serve of stimulus and response moves back and forth in the same manner as a tennis match, only this match is played at very high speed with multiple volleys.

Not only are these extremes doing a rapid subjective objective dance; the two sides of the brain are also communicating on many levels, instantaneously sending masses of information volleying back and forth across the "net" of the corpus callosum, the central area in the fissure of the brain that facilitates communication between both sides.

These multichannel multifunctional energy exchanges happen everywhere throughout our bodies and minds, even down to the cellular and atomic level in everything from neurotransmitters down to cellular respiration, the process that living organisms use to turn food into the energy they need for survival. Cellular respiration can be summarized by the equation:

Organic compounds + oxygen --> carbon dioxide + water + energy

Food contains important organic compounds that have energy stored in their bonds that our bodies need to extract into the usable form of the molecule ATP, or adenosine triphosphate, a form of energy used by all living things.

All of these manifestations of energy move directly from one pole to the other as direct current, or more commonly as alternating back and forth in oscillations that constitute vibration about a central equilibrium point characterized as a zero point between positive and negative poles.

HOW WE PERCEIVE REALITY
IN THE PHYSICAL WORLD

In a mechanical medium sound vibration is perceived in the motion of a tuning fork, a reed in a woodwind instrument, a harmonica, or the cone of a loudspeaker. In the audio spectrum, sound or pressure waves are generated by the previously mentioned vibrating structures, and in our own bodies by the vocal cords, our main transmitting instruments of communication. These pressure waves induce vibration in the structures of our ear drums, our primary mode of receiving communication.

Hearing range describes the range of frequencies that can be heard by humans and other animals. The human range is commonly limited to 20 to 20,000 Hz while several animal species can hear frequencies well beyond the range of human hearing. Some dolphins and bats can hear frequencies up to 100,000 Hz. Elephants can hear sounds at 14–16 Hz, while some whales can hear infrasonic sounds as low as 7 Hz (in water).

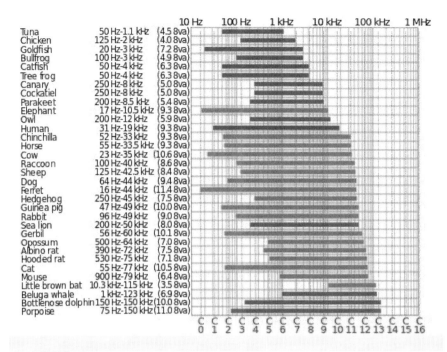

Logarithmic chart of the hearing ranges of some animals

We have two ears, one on each side of our head, allowing us to get a relative 360 degree input from this sense to alert us to what is going on around us - even in the dark, but there is obviously much going on around us that we have no ability to perceive or have any awareness of.

Moving closer to the center of our head, our two eyes are set below our forehead directed in front of us the same way that a predator's eyes are.

We perceive in the visible spectrum, the portion of the electromagnetic spectrum visible to the human eye. Electromagnetic radiation in this range is called visible light or simply light. A typical human eye will respond to wavelengths from about 390 to 700 nm. In terms of frequency, this corresponds to a band in the vicinity of 430–770 THz.

This spectrum does not contain all the colors that human eye and brain can distinguish. Unsaturated colors like pink or purple variations like magenta are absent because they can be made only by a mix of multiple wavelengths. Colors containing only one wavelength are also called pure or spectral colors.

Visible wavelengths pass through the "optical window", the region of the electromagnetic spectrum that allows wavelengths to pass largely unattenuated through the Earth's atmosphere. An example of this phenomenon is that clean air scatters blue light more than red wavelengths, and so the midday sky appears blue. The optical window is also referred to as the "visible window" because it overlaps the human visible response spectrum. The near infrared (NIR) window lies just out of the human vision, as well as the Medium Wavelength IR (MWIR) window, and the Long Wavelength or Far Infrared (LWIR or FIR) window, although other animals may experience them.

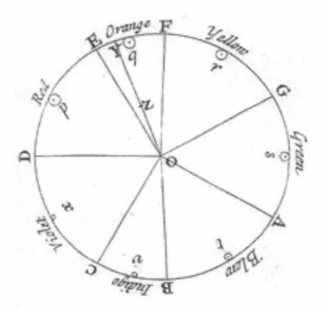

Newton's Color Circle

Newton's color circle shows the colors he associated with musical notes which might help explain the phenomenon of synesthesia where subjects hear color and see sound. The spectral colors from red to violet are divided by the notes of the musical scale, starting at D. The circle completes a full octave, from D to D. Newton's circle places red at one end of the spectrum next to violet at the other. This reflects the fact that non-spectral purple colors are observed when red and violet light are mixed.

Newton divided the visual color spectrum into seven named colors: red, orange, yellow, green, blue, indigo, and violet. He chose the octave of seven colors out of a belief derived from the ancient Greek sophists of a connection between the colors, the musical notes, the known objects in the solar system, and the days of the week.

The human eye is relatively insensitive to indigo's frequencies, and some people who have otherwise good vision cannot distinguish indigo from blue and violet. For this reason later commentators, including Isaac Asimov suggested that indigo should not be regarded as a color in its own right, but merely as a shade of blue or violet, however the evidence indicates that what Newton meant by "indigo" and "blue" does not correspond to the modern meanings of those color words. Comparing Newton's observation of prismatic colors to a color image of the visible light spectrum shows that "indigo" corresponds to what is today called blue, whereas "blue" corresponds to cyan.

The connection between the visible spectrum and color vision was explored by Thomas Young and Hermann von Helmholtz in the early 19th century. Their theory of color vision correctly proposed that the eye uses three distinct receptors to perceive color.

Many other species can see light within frequencies outside the human "visible spectrum". Bees and many other insects can detect ultraviolet light, which helps them find nectar in flowers. Plant species that depend on insect pollination may owe reproductive success to their appearance in ultraviolet light rather than how colorful they appear to humans. Birds can also see into the ultraviolet (300–400 nm), and some have sex-dependent markings on their plumage that are visible only in the ultraviolet range.

Many animals that can see into the ultraviolet range cannot see red light or any other reddish wavelengths. Bees' visible spectrum ends at about 590 nm, just before the orange wavelengths start, while birds can see some red wavelengths, although not as far into the light spectrum as humans. The popular belief that the common goldfish is the only animal that can see both infrared and ultraviolet light is incorrect, because goldfish cannot see infrared light. Similarly, dogs are often thought to be color blind but they have been shown to be sensitive to colors, though not as many as humans.

Colors produced by visible light of a narrow band of wavelengths (monochromatic light) are called pure spectral colors. The various color ranges that are indicated in the following illustration are an approximation of these: The spectrum is continuous, with no clear boundaries between one color and the next.

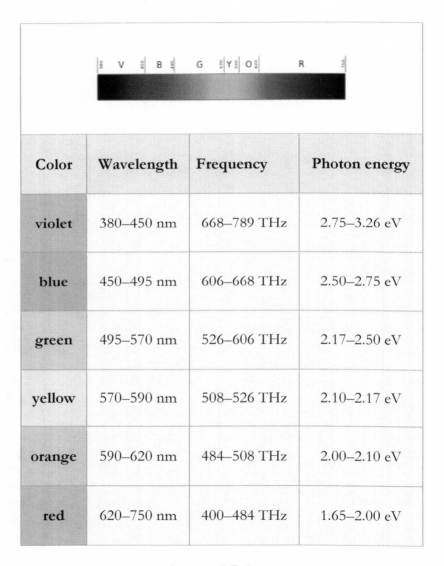

Color	Wavelength	Frequency	Photon energy
violet	380–450 nm	668–789 THz	2.75–3.26 eV
blue	450–495 nm	606–668 THz	2.50–2.75 eV
green	495–570 nm	526–606 THz	2.17–2.50 eV
yellow	570–590 nm	508–526 THz	2.10–2.17 eV
orange	590–620 nm	484–508 THz	2.00–2.10 eV
red	620–750 nm	400–484 THz	1.65–2.00 eV

Spectral Colors

Moving still inward, in the center of our forward facing sensory organs is our protruding nose, which along with our mouth allows us to breathe, as well as function as our organ of smell. Many animals, particularly dogs and bears that have acute sense of smell have longer extended snouts that they literally follow to survive. This organ is the site of specialized sensory receptor cells that transduce chemical substances and generate biological signals that may be in the form of an action potential if the chemoreceptor is a neuron, or in the form of a neurotransmitter that can activate a nearby nerve fiber if the chemosensor is a specialized sensory receptor cell like the taste receptor in a taste bud that forms the sense of smell.

Olfaction has many purposes, such as the detection of hazards, pheremones, and food, and it integrates with other senses to form the sense of flavor. Olfaction occurs when odorants bind to specific sites on olfactory receptors located in the nasal cavity. Glomeruli aggregate signals from these receptors and transmit them to the olfactory bulb where the sensory input interacts with parts of the brain responsible for smell identification, memory, and emotion. Often, land organisms have separate olfaction systems for smell and taste while water-dwelling organisms typically have only one system.

In vertebrates smells are sensed by olfactory sensory neurons in the olfactory epithelium which is made up of at least six morphologically and biochemically different cell types. The proportion of olfactory epithelium compared to respiratory epithelium (not innervated, or supplied with nerves) gives an indication of the animal's olfactory sensitivity. Humans have about 10 cm^2 (1.6 sq in) of olfactory epithelium, whereas some dogs have 170 cm^2 (26 sq in). A dog's olfactory epithelium is also considerably more densely innervated, with a hundred times more receptors per square centimeter.

In insects smells are sensed by olfactory sensory neurons in the chemosensory sensilla which are present in insect antenna, palps, and tarsa, but also on other parts of the insect body. Odorants penetrate into the cuticle pores of chemosensory sensilla and get in contact with insect odorant-binding proteins before activating the sensory neurons.

Many animals including most mammals and reptiles, but not humans, have two distinct and segregated olfactory systems: a main olfactory system, which detects volatile stimuli, and an accessory olfactory system, which detects fluid-phase stimuli. Behavioral evidence suggests that these fluid-phase stimuli often function as pheromones, although pheromones can also be detected by the main olfactory system. In the accessory olfactory system stimuli are detected by the vomeronasal organ, located in the vomer, between the nose and the mouth. Snakes use it to smell prey, sticking their tongue out and touching it to the organ. Some mammals like dogs make a facial expression called flehmen to direct stimuli to this organ.

The process by which olfactory information is coded in the brain to allow for proper perception is still being researched and is not completely understood. When an odorant is detected by receptors they in a sense break the odorant down, and the brain puts it back together for identification and perception.

Recent research suggests that the average individual is capable of distinguishing over one trillion unique odors. Researchers tested the psychophysical responses to combinations of over 128 unique odor molecules with combinations composed of up to 30 different component molecules noted that this estimate is "conservative", and that some subjects of their research might be capable of deciphering between a thousand trillion odorants, adding that their worst performer could probably still distinguish between 80 million scents. Authors of the study concluded that the human olfactory system with its hundreds of different olfactory receptors far outperforms the other senses in the number of physically different stimuli it can discriminate.

Flavor perception is an aggregation of auditory, taste, haptic, and smell sensory information. Haptic perception is the ability "to grasp something". Perception in this case is achieved through the active exploration of surfaces and objects by a moving subject, as opposed to passive contact by a static subject during *tactile perception*.

During the process of mastication, the tongue manipulates food to release odorants. These odorants enter the nasal cavity during exhalation. The olfaction of food has the sensation of being in the mouth because of co-activation of the motor cortex and olfactory epithelium during mastication.

In the plant and animal kingdoms the tendrils of plants are especially sensitive to airborne volatile organic compounds. Parasites such as dodder make use of this in locating their preferred hosts and locking on to them. The emission of volatile compounds is detected when foliage is browsed by animals. Threatened plants are able to take defensive chemical measures such as moving tannin compounds to their foliage.

The importance and sensitivity of smell varies among different organisms; most mammals have a good sense of smell, whereas most birds do not, except the tubenoses like petrels and albatrosses, certain species of vultures, and kiwis. Among mammals it is well developed in the carnivores and ungulates which always have to be aware of each other, and in those that smell for their food such as moles. Having a strong sense of smell is referred to as *macrosmatic*.

It is estimated that dogs have an olfactory sense that is approximately ten thousand to a hundred thousand times more acute than a human's. This does not mean they are overwhelmed by smells our noses can detect; rather it means they can discern a molecular presence when it is in much greater dilution in the carrier, air.

Scenthounds as a group can smell one to ten-million times more acutely than a human and bloodhounds have the keenest sense of smell of any dogs with noses ten to one-hundred-million times more sensitive than a human's. They were bred for the specific purpose of tracking humans, and can detect a scent trail a few days old. The second-most-sensitive nose is possessed by the Basset Hound which was bred to track and hunt rabbits and other small animals.

Bears, like the Silvertip Grizzly found in parts of North America have a sense of smell seven times stronger than that of the bloodhound, essential for locating food underground. Using their elongated claws, bears dig deep trenches in search of burrowing animals and nests as well as roots, bulbs, and insects. Bears can detect the scent of food from up to eighteen miles away, and because of their immense size, they often scavenge new kills, driving away predators, including packs of wolves and human hunters in the process.

Fish also have a well-developed sense of smell, even though they inhabit an aquatic environment. Salmon utilize their sense of smell to identify and return to their home stream waters. Catfish use their sense of smell to identify other individual catfish and to maintain a social hierarchy. Many fish use the sense of smell to identify mating partners or to alert to the presence of food.

Mammals have about a thousand genes that are coded for odor reception. Of these only a portion are functional. Humans have far fewer active odor receptor genes than other primates and other mammals. In mammals each olfactory receptor neuron expresses only one functional odor receptor. Odor receptor nerve cells function like a key–lock system: if the airborne molecules of a certain chemical fit into the lock, the nerve cell responds. There are at present a number of competing theories regarding the mechanism of odor coding and perception. According to the shape theory, each receptor detects a feature of the odor molecule.

The weak-shape theory, known as the odotope theory suggests that different receptors detect only small pieces of molecules, and these minimal inputs are combined to form a larger olfactory perception similar to the way visual perception is built up of smaller, information-poor sensations combined and refined to create a detailed overall perception. Researchers have found that a functional relationship exists between molecular volume of odorants and the olfactory neural response.

The vibration theory proposed by Luca Turin posits that odor receptors detect the frequencies of vibrations of odor molecules in the infrared range by quantum tunnelling. Although there is no theory yet that explains olfactory perception completely, the fact that seeing, hearing, and touch are frequency dependent lend weight to the vibration theory.

ALL PATHS LEAD TO SUSTENANCE

All of our senses, including our sense of touch ultimately bring us to the mouth, our organ of sustenance located below and intimately connected to the nose, which is directed by retronasal smell, retronasal olfaction, or mouth smell, giving us the ability to perceive the flavor dimensions of foods and drinks. Retronasal smell is a sensory modality that produces flavor best described as a combination of traditional smell (orthonasal smell) and taste modalities that create flavor from smell molecules in foods or drinks shunting up through the nasal passages as one is chewing. When people use the term smell, they are usually referring to orthonasal smell, or the perception of smell molecules that enter through the nose and up the nasal passages. Retronasal smell is critical for experiencing the *flavor* of foods and drinks. Flavor should be contrasted with taste, which refers to five specific dimensions: (1) sweet, (2) salty, (3) bitter, (4) sour, and (5) umami. Perceiving anything beyond these five dimensions, like distinguishing the flavor of an apple from a pear requires retronasal smell.

Taste in the gustatory system allows humans to distinguish between safe and harmful food, and to gauge foods nutritional value. Digestive enzymes in saliva dissolve food into base chemicals that are washed over the papillae and detected as tastes by the taste buds. The tongue is covered with thousands of small bumps called papillae, which are visible to the naked eye. Within each papilla are hundreds of taste buds. The exception to this are the filiform papillae that do not contain taste buds. There are between 2000 and 5000 taste buds located on the back and front of the tongue. Others are located on the roof, sides, the back of the mouth, and in the throat. Each taste bud contains 50 to 100 taste receptor cells.

Bitter food generally tasted unpleasant, while sour, salty, sweet, and meaty tasting foods provide pleasurable sensations. The five specific tastes received by taste receptors are saltiness, sweetness, bitterness, sourness, and *umami*, which means 'delicious' in Japanese and is sometimes translated as "savory" in English. As of the early twentieth century, Western physiologists and psychologists believed there were four basic tastes: sweetness, sourness, saltiness, and bitterness. At that time umami was not identified, but now a large number of authorities recognize it as the fifth taste.

Sour and salt tastes can be pleasant in small quantities, but in larger quantities they become more and more unpleasant to taste. For sour taste this is presumably because the sour taste can signal under-ripe fruit, rotten meat, and other spoiled foods which can be dangerous to the body because of bacteria that grow in such media. Additionally, sour taste signals acids which can cause tissue damage.

The bitter taste is almost universally unpleasant to humans because many nitrogenous organic molecules have a pharmacological effect on humans that taste bitter, including caffeine, nicotine, and strychnine, which respectively compose the stimulants in coffee, cigarettes, and as the active compound in many pesticides.

It appears that some psychological process allows humans to overcome their innate aversion to bitter taste, as caffeinated drinks are widely consumed and enjoyed around the world. Additionally, many common medicines have a bitter taste if chewed, indicating that the gustatory system most likely interprets these compounds as poisons. In this manner, the unpleasant reaction to the bitter taste is a last-line warning system before the compound is ingested and can do damage.

Sweet taste signals the presence of carbohydrates in solution. Since carbohydrates have a very high calorie count (saccharides have many bonds, therefore much energy), they are desirable to the human body which evolved to seek out the highest calorie intake foods. Carbohydrates are used as direct energy (sugars) and storage of energy (glycogen), however there are many non-carbohydrate molecules that trigger a sweet response, leading to the development of artificial sweeteners, including saccharin, sucralose, and aspartame. It is still unclear how these substances activate the sweet receptors and what adaptational significance this has had.

The umami taste was identified by Japanese chemist Kikunae Ikeda of Tokyo Imperial University signals the presence of the amino acid L-glutamate, triggers a pleasurable response encouraging the intake of peptides and proteins. The amino acids in proteins are used in the body to build muscles and organs, transport molecules (hemoglobin), antibodies, and the organic catalysts known as enzymes. These are all critical molecules, and as such it is important to have a steady supply of amino acids, hence the pleasurable response to their presence in the mouth.

Taste is a form of chemoreception that occurs in the five different types of specialized taste receptors in the mouth. Each receptor has a different manner of sensory transduction: that is, of detecting the presence of a certain compound and starting an action potential that alerts the brain.

Where the head is the center of perception for four of our senses, the fifth sense is centered in the body, our primary organ of feeling, and at the center of that is our heart which is considered the center of feeling and emotion.

Ancient shamanic cultures saw the heart as the true center of their personal universe that functioned as the portal connecting them through the sun of our local solar system through multiple permutations all the way back to the infinite source of the great mystery.

Our heads and our hearts are often at odds with each other for a number of reasons which will be explored in a later chapter, but for our present discussion, continuing our inward bound tour to our true center brings us to our tactile senses that literally cover our whole body with greater concentrations of nerve endings located at critical points like our fingertips and face.

This multifaceted and pervasive network is a complex system of sensory neurons and pathways known as our somatosensory system that responds to changes at the surface or inside the body. The axon nerve fibers of sensory neurons connect and respond to various sensory receptor cells that are activated by different stimuli like heat and pain, giving a functional name to the responding sensory neuron such as thermoreceptors that carry information about temperature changes, making them vibratory sensors in that heat is a form of energy produced when molecules increase their rate of oscillation.

Other types of cells include mechanoreceptors, chemoreceptors, and nociceptors that send signals along a sensory nerve to the spinal cord where they are processed by other sensory neurons and relayed to the brain for further processing. Sensory receptors are found all over the body including the skin, epithelial tissues, muscles, bones, and joints, internal organs, and the cardiovascular system.

Somatic senses are sometimes referred to as somesthetic senses with the understanding that somesthesis includes the sense of touch, proprioception (sense of position and movement), and (depending on usage) haptic perception. This form of haptic perception is related to the concept of extended physiological proprioception, according to which, when a tool such as a stick is used, perceptual experience is transparently transferred to the end of the tool. In this case haptic perception relies on the forces experienced during touch. Four mechanoreceptors in the skin each respond to different stimuli for short or long periods.

Merkel cell nerve endings are found in the basal epidermis and hair follicles. They react to low vibrations (5–15 Hz) and deep static touch such as shapes and edges. Due to a small receptive field of extremely detailed information they are used in areas like fingertips the most. They are not covered (shelled) and thus respond to pressures over long periods.

Tactile corpuscles react to moderate vibration (10–50 Hz) and light touch and are located in the dermal papillae. Due to their reactivity they are primarily located in fingertips and lips and respond in quick action potentials, unlike Merkel. They are responsible for the ability to read Braille and feel gentle stimuli.

Lamellar corpuscles determine gross touch and distinguish rough and soft substances. They react in quick action potentials, especially to vibrations around 250 Hz (even up to centimeters away). They are the most sensitive to vibrations and have large receptor fields. Pacinian reacts only to sudden stimuli so pressures like clothes that are always compressing their shape are quickly ignored.

Bulbous corpuscles react slowly and respond to sustained skin stretch, and are responsible for the feeling of object slippage and play a major role in the kinesthetic sense and control of finger position and movement. Merkel and bulbous cells (slow-response) are myelinated; the rest (fast-response) are not. All of these receptors are activated upon pressures that squish their shape causing an action potential.

The receptor for the sense of balance resides in the vestibular system in the ear for the three-dimensional orientation of the head, and by inference, the rest of the body. Balance is also mediated by the kinesthetic reflex fed by proprioception that senses the relative location of the rest of the body to the head. In addition, proprioception estimates the location of objects which are sensed by the visual system providing confirmation of the place of those objects relative to the body as input to the mechanical reflexes of the body.

The somatosensory cortex encodes incoming sensory information from receptors all over the body. Affective touch is a type of sensory information that elicits an emotional reaction and is usually social in nature, such as a physical human touch. This type of information is coded differently than other sensory information. Intensity of affective touch is still encoded in the primary somatosensory cortex, but the feeling of pleasantness associated with affective touch activates the anterior cingulate cortex more than the primary somatosensory cortex. Functional magnetic resonance imaging (fMRI) data shows that increased blood oxygen level contrast (BOLD) signal in the anterior cingulate cortex as well as the prefrontal cortex is highly correlated with pleasantness scores of an affective touch. Inhibitory transcranial magnetic stimulation (TMS) of the primary somatosensory cortex inhibits the perception of affective touch intensity, but not affective touch pleasantness.

THE SYMPHONY WITHIN

Neural oscillations or brainwaves are rhythmic or repetitive neural activity occurring in the central nervous system. Neural tissue can generate oscillatory activity in many ways, driven either by mechanisms within individual neurons or by interactions between neurons. In individual neurons, oscillations can appear either as oscillations in membrane potential or as rhythmic patterns of action potentials which produce oscillatory activation of post-synaptic neurons.

At the level of neural ensembles, synchronized activity of large numbers of neurons can give rise to macroscopic oscillations which can be observed in an electroencephalogram. Oscillatory activity in groups of neurons generally arise from feedback connections between neurons that result in the synchronization of their firing patterns. The interaction between neurons can also give rise to oscillations at a different frequency than the firing frequency of individual neurons. A well-known example of macroscopic neural oscillations is alpha activity.

Alpha waves are neural oscillations in the frequency range of 7.5–12.5 Hz arising from synchronous and coherent (in phase or constructive) electrical activity of thalamic pacemaker cells in humans, and are one type of brain wave that can be detected either by electroencephalography(EEG) or magnetoencephalography (MEG). They predominantly originate from the occipital lobe during wakeful relaxation with closed eyes. Alpha waves are reduced with open eyes, drowsiness, and sleep.

Some possible roles of neural oscillations include feature binding, information transfer mechanisms, and the generation of rhythmic motor output. Oscillatory activity in the brain is widely observed at different levels of organization and is thought to play a key role in processing neural information.

Neural oscillations are observed throughout the central nervous system at all levels, and include spike trains, local field potentials, and large-scale oscillations which can be measured by EEG. In general, oscillations can be characterized by their frequency, amplitude, and phase. In large-scale oscillations, amplitude changes come from changes in synchronization within a neural ensemble, also referred to as local synchronization.

In addition to local synchronization, oscillatory activity of distant neural structures (single neurons or neural ensembles) can synchronize. Neural oscillations and synchronization have been linked to many cognitive functions such as information transfer, perception, motor control, and memory.

The first discovered and best-known frequency band is alpha activity (7.5–12.5 Hz) that can be detected from the occipital lobe during relaxed wakefulness and increases when the eyes are closed.

Other recognized frequency bands are: delta (1–4 Hz), theta (4–8 Hz), beta (13–30 Hz) and gamma (30–70 Hz) frequencies. Faster rhythms like gamma activity have been linked to cognitive processing. Indeed, EEG signals change dramatically during sleep and show a transition from faster frequencies to increasingly slower frequencies like alpha waves. Different sleep stages are commonly characterized by their spectral content. Consequently, neural oscillations have been linked to cognitive states, such as awareness and consciousness.

Neurons can generate rhythmic patterns of action potentials or spikes, and some types of neurons have the tendency to fire at particular frequencies, which are referred to as *resonators*. Bursting is another form of rhythmic spiking. Spiking patterns are considered fundamental for information coding in the brain. If numerous neurons spike in synchrony, they can give rise to oscillations in local field potentials.

Neural oscillations are commonly studied from a mathematical framework and belong to the field of "neurodynamics", an area of research in the cognitive sciences that places strong focus on the dynamic character of neural activity in describing brain function. It considers the brain to be a dynamical system and uses differential equations to describe how neural activity evolves over time. In particular, it aims to relate dynamic patterns of brain activity to cognitive functions like perception and memory.

The functions of neural oscillations are wide-ranging and vary for different types of oscillatory activity. Examples are the generation of rhythmic activity like a heartbeat and the neural binding of sensory features in perception, like the shape and color of an object. Oscillatory activity can also be used to control external devices in brain–computer interfaces, where subjects can control an external device by changing the amplitude of particular brain rhythmics.

Oscillatory activity is observed throughout the central nervous system at all levels of organization. Three different levels have been widely recognized: the micro-scale (activity of a single neuron), the meso-scale (activity of a local group of neurons) and the macro-scale (activity of different brain regions.

Neurons generate action potentials resulting from changes in the electric membrane potential and can generate multiple action potentials in sequence forming so-called spike trains which are the basis for neural coding and information transfer in the brain. Spike trains can form all kinds of patterns, such as rhythmic spiking and bursting, and often display oscillatory activity.

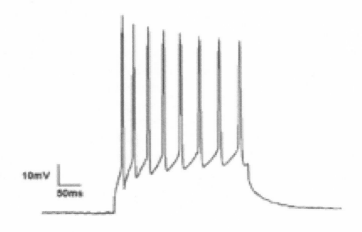

**Tonic firing pattern of single neuron
showing rhythmic spiking activity**

Neural ensembles can generate oscillatory activity endogenously through local interactions between excitatory and inhibitory neurons. In particular, inhibitory interneurons play an important role in producing neural ensemble synchrony by generating a narrow window for effective excitation and rhythmically modulating the firing rate of excitatory neurons.

Neural oscillation can also arise from interactions between different brain areas coupled through the structural connectome. Because all brain areas are bidirectionally coupled, these connections between brain areas form feedback loops. Positive feedback loops tend to cause oscillatory activity where frequency is inversely related to the delay time. An example of such a feedback loop is the connections between the thalamus and cortex. This thalamocortical network is able to generate oscillatory activity known as recurrent thalamo-cortical resonance. The thalamocortical network plays an important role in the generation of alpha activity.

In a whole-brain network model with realistic anatomical connectivity and propagation delays between 90 brain areas, oscillations in the beta frequency range emerge from the partial synchronisation of subsets of brain areas oscillating in the gamma-band (generated at the mesoscopic level). This occurs because synchronisation in the presence of time delays reduces the oscillation frequency.

In addition to periodic spiking, subthreshold membrane potential oscillations such as resonance behavior that does not result in action potentials, may also contribute to oscillatory activity by facilitating synchronous activity of neighboring neurons. Like pacemaker neurons in central pattern generators, subtypes of cortical cells fire bursts of spikes rhythmically at preferred frequencies. Bursting neurons have the potential to serve as pacemakers for synchronous network oscillations, and bursts of spikes may underlie or enhance neuronal resonance.

If a group of neurons engages in synchronized oscillatory activity, the neural ensemble can be mathematically represented as a single oscillator. Different neural ensembles are coupled through long-range connections and form a network of weakly coupled oscillators at the next spatial scale. Weakly coupled oscillators can generate a range of dynamics including oscillatory activity.

Long-range connections between different brain structures, such as the thalamus and the cortex involve time-delays due to the finite conduction velocity of axons. Because most connections are reciprocal, they form feed-back loops that support oscillatory activity. Oscillations recorded from multiple cortical areas can become synchronized to form large scale brain networks. Coherent activity of large-scale brain activity can also form dynamic links between brain areas required for the integration of distributed information.

In addition to fast direct synaptic interactions between neurons forming a network, oscillatory activity is also modulated by neurotransmitters that are firing on a much slower time scale. GABA concentration has been shown to be positively correlated with frequency of oscillations in induced stimuli.

A number of nuclei in the brainstem have diffuse projections throughout the brain influencing concentration levels of neurotransmitters like norepinephrine, acetylcholine and serotonin. These neurotransmitter systems affect physiological states like wakefulness or arousal, and have a pronounced effect on amplitude of different brain waves such as alpha activity.

Oscillations can often be described and analyzed using mathematics and mathematicians have in fact identified several dynamical mechanisms that generate rhythmicity. Among the most important are harmonic (linear) oscillators, limit cycle oscillators, and delayed-feedback oscillators. Harmonic oscillations appear frequently in nature—examples are sound waves, the motion of a pendulum, and vibrations of every sort. They generally arise when a physical system is perturbed by a small degree from a minimum-energy state, and are well understood mathematically. Noise-driven harmonic oscillators realistically simulate alpha rhythm in waking EEG as well as slow waves and spindles in sleep EEG.

Linear oscillators and limit-cycle oscillators qualitatively differ in terms of how they respond to fluctuations in input. In a linear oscillator the frequency is more or less constant but the amplitude can vary greatly. In a limit-cycle oscillator the amplitude tends to be more or less constant, but the frequency can vary greatly. A heartbeat is an example of a limit-cycle oscillation in that the frequency of beats varies widely, while each individual beat continues to pump about the same amount of blood.

A neural network model describes a population of physically interconnected neurons or a group of disparate neurons whose inputs or signaling targets define a recognizable circuit. These models aim to describe how the dynamics of neural circuitry arise from interactions between individual neurons. Local interactions between neurons can result in the synchronization of spiking activity and form the basis of oscillatory activity. In particular, models of interacting pyramidal cells and inhibitory interneurons have been shown to generate brain rhythms like gamma activity.

Spontaneous activity is brain activity in the absence of an explicit task, such as sensory input or motor output, and is also referred to as resting-state activity as opposed to activity that is induced by sensory stimuli or motor responses. Spontaneous activity is considered to play a crucial role during brain development, such as in network formation and synaptogenesis, and may be informative regarding the current mental state of the person (e.g. wakefulness, alertness) and is often used in sleep research. Certain types of oscillatory activity like alpha waves are part of spontaneous activity.

Ongoing brain activity also has an important role in perception, as it interacts with activity related to incoming stimuli. EEG studies suggest that visual perception is dependent on both the phase and amplitude of cortical oscillations as in the case when the amplitude and phase of alpha activity at the moment of visual stimulation predicts whether a weak stimulus will be perceived by the subject.

In response to input, a neuron or neuronal ensemble may change the frequency at which it oscillates, thus changing the rate at which it spikes. Often, a neuron's firing rate depends on the summed activity it receives. Frequency changes are also commonly observed in central pattern generators and directly relate to the speed of motor activities like step frequency in walking, however changes in *relative* oscillation frequency between different brain areas is not so common because the frequency of oscillatory activity is often related to time delays between brain areas.

Next to evoked activity, neural activity related to stimulus processing can result in induced activity which refers to modulation in ongoing brain activity induced by processing of stimuli or movement preparation reflecting an indirect response in contrast to evoked responses. A well-studied type of induced activity is amplitude change in oscillatory activity such as when gamma activity increases during increased mental activity during object representation.

Increases in oscillatory activity are often referred to as event-related synchronization while decreases are referred to as event-related desynchronization. Neural synchronization can be modulated by task constraints such as attention and is thought to play a role in feature binding, neuronal communication, and motor coordination.

Synchronized firing of neurons also forms the basis of periodic motor commands for rhythmic movements which are produced by a group of interacting neurons that form a network, called a central pattern generator. Central pattern generators are neuronal circuits that when activated can produce rhythmic motor patterns in the absence of sensory or descending inputs that carry specific timing information. Examples are walking, breathing, and swimming,

Neuronal spiking is generally considered the basis for information transfer in the brain. For such a transfer, information needs to be coded in a spiking pattern.

Perceiving different odors leads to different subsets of neurons firing on different sets of oscillatory cycles. These oscillations can be disrupted by GABA blocker picrotoxin, and the disruption of the oscillatory synchronization leads to impairment of behavioral discrimination of chemically similar odorants in bees and to more similar responses across odors in downstream β-lobe neurons.

Oscillations have been commonly reported in the motor system. Pfurtscheller and colleagues found a reduction in alpha (8–12 Hz) and beta (13–30 Hz) oscillations in EEG activity when subjects made a movement. Using intra-cortical recordings, similar changes in oscillatory activity were found in the motor cortex when monkeys performed motor acts that required significant attention.

In addition, oscillations at spinal level become synchronized to beta oscillations in the motor cortex during constant muscle activation as determined by cortico-muscular coherence. Likewise, muscle activity of different muscles reveals inter-muscular coherence at multiple distinct frequencies reflecting the underlying neural circuitry involved in motor coordination.

Cortical oscillations propagate as travelling waves across the surface of the motor cortex along dominant spatial axes characteristic of the local circuitry of the motor cortex. It has been proposed that motor commands in the form of travelling waves can be spatially filtered by the descending fibers to selectively control muscle force. Simulations have shown that ongoing wave activity in the cortex can elicit steady muscle force with physiological levels of EEG-EMG coherence.

Neural oscillations, in particular theta activity, are extensively linked to memory function. Theta rhythms are very strong in rodent hippocampi and entorhinal cortex during learning and memory retrieval and are believed to be vital to the induction of long-term potentiation, a potential cellular mechanism for learning and memory. Coupling between theta and gamma activity is thought to be vital for memory functions including episodic memory. Tight coordination of single-neuron spikes with local theta oscillations is linked to successful memory formation in humans, as more stereotyped spiking predicts better memory.

Sleep is a naturally recurring state characterized by reduced or absent consciousness and it proceeds in distinct cycles of rapid eye movement (REM) and non-rapid eye movement (NREM) sleep. The normal order of sleep stages is N1 → N2 → N3 → N2 → REM. Sleep stages are characterized by spectral content of EEG: for instance, stage N1 refers to the transition of the brain from alpha waves (common in the awake state) to theta waves, whereas stage N3 (deep or slow-wave sleep) is characterized by the presence of delta waves.

GETTING IN TUNE

By learning to master the energies of altered states shamans embrace a multitude of experiences that alter their perception of reality by changing their subjective experience the same way a radio receiver changes the station it receives by tuning in to different carrier frequencies. The concepts of resonance and synchronization play a big part in shamanic thought and experience.

In physics, resonance is a phenomenon in which a vibrating system or external force drives another system to oscillate with greater amplitude at specific frequencies.

Frequencies at which the response amplitude is a relative maximum are known as the system's resonant frequencies or resonance frequencies, and at resonant frequencies, small periodic driving forces have the ability to produce large amplitude oscillations, due to the storage of vibrational energy.

Resonance occurs when a system is able to store and easily transfer energy between two or more different storage modes such as kinetic energy and potential energy in the case of a simple pendulum, however, there are some losses from cycle to cycle, called damping. When damping is small, the resonant frequency is approximately equal to the natural frequency of the system, which is a frequency of unforced vibrations. Some systems have multiple, distinct, resonant frequencies.

Resonance phenomena occur with all types of vibrations or waves, including those that occur in mechanical resonance, acoustic resonance, electromagnetic resonance, and in nuclear magnetic resonance (NMR), as well as in electron spin resonance (ESR), and resonance of quantum wave functions. Resonant systems can be used to generate vibrations of a specific frequency such as with musical instruments, or pick out specific frequencies from a complex vibration containing many frequencies as in filters.

The term *resonance* (from Latin *resonantia*, 'echo', from *resonare*, 'resound') originates from the field of acoustics, and is particularly observed in musical instruments, such as when strings vibrate and produce sound without direct excitation by the player.

The name of the musical note "Re" in the solfège scale may come from the word *resonare*, as it appears in a religious anthem for John the Baptist in Latin. This was due to the naming of musical notes by the Italian medieval scholar Guido of Arezzo.

Resonance occurs widely in nature and is exploited in many man made devices, and it is the mechanism by which virtually all sinusoidal waves and vibrations are generated. Many sounds we hear, such as when hard objects of metal, glass, or wood are struck, are caused by brief resonant vibrations in the object. Light and other short wavelength electromagnetic radiation is produced by resonance on an atomic scale, such as electrons in atoms.

Mechanical resonance is the tendency of a mechanical system to absorb more energy when the frequency of its oscillations matches the system's natural frequency of vibration.

Acoustic resonance is a branch of mechanical resonance that is concerned with the mechanical vibrations across the frequency range of human hearing. In other words sound. When sound waves strike a wall in an auditorium the sound reacts to various frequency energy dependent on the composition and various geometrical degrees present in the wall.

Acoustic resonance is an important consideration for instrument builders, as most acoustic instruments use resonators like the strings and body of a violin, the length of tube in a flute, and the shape of and tension on a drum membrane.

Electrical resonance always occurs within electric circuits at particular resonant frequencies when the impedance of the circuit is at a minimum in a series circuit or at maximum in a parallel circuit, or when the transfer function is at a maximum. Resonance in circuits are used for both transmitting and receiving wireless communications such as in computer networks, television, cell phones, and radio.

In simpler terms, when two or more objects are vibrating at the same frequency there is a maximum exchange of energy between them and they share the same characteristics of that particular energy made evident by their synchronization, which is the coordination of events to operate a system in unison. The familiar conductor of an orchestra serves to keep the orchestra *in time*. Systems operating with all their parts in synchrony are said to be *synchronous* or *in sync*.

In electrical engineering terms, for digital logic and data transfer, a synchronous circuit requires a clock signal. However, the use of the word "clock" in this sense is different from the typical sense of a clock as a device that keeps track of time-of-day.

Synchronization is an emergent property that occurs in a broad range of dynamical systems, including neural signaling, evident in the synchronized activity of neural ensembles that give rise to macroscopic oscillations of Alpha waves, the beating of the heart, and the synchronization of fire-fly light waves.

In groups, synchronization of movement has been shown to increase conformity, cooperation, and trust, but more research on group synchronization is needed to determine its effects on groups as a whole, and on individuals within a group. In dyads -- groups of two people, synchronization has been shown to increase affiliation, self-esteem, compassion and altruistic behavior, and increase rapport.

During arguments, synchrony between the arguing pair has been noted to decrease, however it is not clear whether this is due to the change in emotion or other factors. There is evidence to show that movement synchronization requires other people to cause its beneficial effects, as the effect on affiliation does not occur when one of the dyad is synchronizing their movements to something outside of the dyad. This is known as interpersonal synchrony.

Research in this area detailing the positive effects of synchrony have attributed this to synchrony alone, however many of the experiments incorporate a shared intention to achieve synchrony. The Reinforcement of Cooperation Model suggests that perception of synchrony leads to reinforcement that cooperation is occurring, which leads to the pro-social effects of synchrony.

If synchronization occurs in a broad range of dynamical systems, including mechanical, acoustic, electrical, and neural signaling, and has been shown to increase conformity, cooperation, pro-social effects and trust in groups, is it possible to observe this phenomenon in different states of consciousness that may provide access to other realms of experience?

Can we synchronize our inner universe so that it comes into resonance not only internally, but externally in the world and people around us, as well as in the plant and animal kingdoms along with other normally invisible energies that surround and inform us?

MORPHIC RESONANCE AND MORPHIC FIELDS

Biologist and author Rupert Sheldrake is best known for his hypothesis of morphic fields and morphic resonance that leads to a vision of a living developing universe with its own inherent memory. Over the course of fifteen years of research on plant development he came to the conclusion that for understanding the development of plants, their morphogenesis, genes and gene products were not enough. Morphogenesis also depends on organizing fields. How *does* a massive oak grow out of an acorn?

The same arguments apply to the development of animals. Since the 1920s many developmental biologists have proposed that biological organization depends on fields, variously called biological fields, developmental fields, positional fields, or morphogenetic fields.

Many organisms live as free cells, including many yeasts, bacteria and amoebas. Some form complex mineral skeletons, as in diatoms and radiolarians. Just making the right proteins at the right times cannot explain the complex skeletons of such structures without many other forces coming into play, including the organizing activity of cell membranes and microtubules.

Most developmental biologists accept the need for a holistic or integrative conception of living organization, otherwise biology will go on floundering, even drowning in oceans of data, as yet more genomes are sequenced, genes are cloned, and proteins are characterized.

Sheldrake suggests that morphogenetic fields work by imposing patterns on otherwise random or indeterminate patterns of activity as is the case when they cause microtubules to crystallize in one part of the cell rather than another, even though the subunits from which they are made are present throughout the cell.

Morphogenetic fields are not fixed, they evolve. The fields of Afghan hounds and poodles have become different from those of their common ancestors, wolves. How are these fields inherited? It's been postulated that they are transmitted from past members of the species through a kind of non-local resonance, called morphic resonance.

The fields organizing the activity of the nervous system are likewise inherited through morphic resonance, conveying a collective, instinctive memory. Each individual both draws upon and contributes to the collective memory of the species, meaning new patterns of behavior can spread more rapidly than would otherwise be possible. As an example, if rats of a particular breed learn a new trick in Harvard, then rats of that breed should be able to learn the same trick faster all over the world. There is evidence from laboratory experiments that this actually happens.

Social groups are also organized by fields, as in schools of fish and flocks of birds. Human societies have memories that are transmitted through the culture of the group, and are most explicitly communicated through the ritual re-enactment of a founding story or myth, as in the Jewish Passover celebration, the Christian Holy Communion and the American thanksgiving dinner, through which the past become present through a kind of resonance with those who have performed the same rituals before.

If we want to stick to the idea of natural laws, we can say that as nature itself evolves, the laws of nature also evolve just as human laws evolve over time, but how would natural laws be remembered or enforced? The law metaphor is embarrassingly anthropomorphic. Habits are less human-centered. Many kinds of organisms have habits, but only humans have laws. The habits of nature depend on non-local similarity reinforcement. Through morphic resonance, the patterns of activity in self-organizing systems are influenced by similar patterns in the past, giving each species and each kind of self-organizing system a collective memory.

Habits are subject to natural selection and the more often they are repeated, the more probable they become, other things being equal. Animals inherit the successful habits of their species as instincts. We inherit bodily, emotional, mental and cultural habits, including the habits of our languages.

The morphic fields of social groups connect members of the group even when they are miles apart, and provide channels of communication through which organisms can stay in touch at a distance, and they help provide an explanation for telepathy. There is good evidence that many species of animals are telepathic, and telepathy seems to be a normal means of animal communication which is normal not paranormal, natural not supernatural, and is common between people, especially those who know each other well.

The morphic fields of mental activity are not confined to the insides of our heads. They extend far beyond our brain though intention and attention. We are already familiar with the idea of fields extending beyond the material objects in which they are rooted, such as when magnetic fields extend beyond the surfaces of magnets, the earth's gravitational field extends far beyond the surface of the earth, keeping the moon in its orbit; and when the fields of a cell phone stretch out far beyond the phone itself. In this same manner, the fields of our minds extend far beyond our brains.

HOW PLANTS AND ANIMALS
COMMUNICATE WITH US

In a shaman's world view, *everything* is energy, and for them the word spirit and energy have the exact same meaning. If you look at things from this perspective, how do plants, animals, and insects communicate with us and each other?

On an olfactory level, plants call out to us from a distance by their varied aromas that form the basis for many scents and perfumes that are attractive to humans, often to the point of stimulating a resonance between lovers. Additionally they are used as powerful tools in aromatherapies to induce recall, reinforce powerful emotion, or simply for the calming quality of their fragrances.

When they affect us in these profound ways, it is because we resonate with them.

On a visual level we are often attracted to them by their stunning beauty, and we display them in our homes and businesses to "brighten things up". It is a long held tradition to bring roses to a romantic partner to show love and as a traditional courting strategy, and we send flowers to commemorate special land mark human occasions like birth, marriage, and death.

These visual and olfactory cues combine to attract pollinators and other synergistic interactions to spread seeds and enhance other survival strategies aided by other species, and this is only what we see in the frequency spectrums that we normally perceive. Who knows what might be happening in the spectrums that other species can perceive that we cannot?

Similarly, in the vegetable kingdom, as shown in the complex interaction of the olfactory and taste receptors, these characteristics combine to help us identify what is healthy to ingest and aid us.

On vision quests and in visionary states, particularly those encountered on strict shamanic plant diets centered around the Ayahuasca brew, subjects imbibe any number and combination of specialized plants to learn from the spirits of the plants by passing through physical, mental, and spiritual ordeals to prove that they are worthy of the gift of knowledge that the plant spirits have to give them.

Each plant and animal has its own spirit, essence, or energy which can be characterized as its own unique personality in the same way that Ayahuasca is universally referred to as "The Mother". It is also the reason why North American Indians don't refer to animals as the bear or the coyote. They say Bear or Coyote as they consider them all to be manifesting the entire essence of their spirit in a grouped manner, similar to bees, ants, and other cooperative colonies, and each one has its own unique energy signature that is treated with equal respect, such as the well-known personality of Coyote the Trickster.

When you ingest a particular plant or plants, especially in a specific environment while on a strict cleansing diet, their effects are strongly felt and enhanced, even more so the longer the diet is continued. During that time participants are subject to the energy field of that plant or plants, which all interact with each other and our bodies and minds in different ways.

The combination of the diet, environment, the plants and other elements affect our brain wave activities and physiologies in a myriad of mysterious ways on physical, psychological, and spiritual levels that we can scarcely comprehend, much less study in any traditional, objective scientific way. The best way to study them is from the outside in through the subjective perceptions they produce in experiences that often transpire on deep non-rational levels of resonance and synchronization with the plants as transmitters in the position of orchestra conductors, and the subjects as receivers, communicating in ways that defy logic and articulation.

An Ayahuasca ceremony is characterized as an individual healing experience in a group setting with much anecdotal evidence supporting sporadic telepathic experiences among participants. The healing circle is referred to as a container to safely hold the energy it generates and attracts so that the participants can be protected while in the vulnerable state necessary for healing.

If a group of people all sat around with their own radios, each tuned to the same station listening to the same song, all of the radios would be playing the same music as one, in sync. If all of the participants in the healing circle tuned in and resonated at the same frequency or frequencies, there is no reason why they would not have similar shared telepathic events.

This learned ability to subject themselves to these diverse natural energies to surrender and discover what mysteries they may reveal puts shamans in the humbling position of being subject to their plant teachers as the conductor transmitters, in spite of the physical or psychological discomfort they may have in the process.

In the Amazon, Ayahuasca is often referred to as *la purga*, because it purges the body and rigorously clears it out through every orifice, including vomiting, defecation, profuse sweating, tear ducts, and the lungs as well as energetically at deep psychological and spiritual levels. Often it is used in conjunction with other intensely purgative plants along with the restricted diet referred to as the *dieta* consisting of boiled rice, oatmeal, or quinoa, baked or boiled unripe bananas, and chicken or fish once a day or less combined with a pitcher a day of a helper plant or plants. There is no salt, no soap, shampoo, toothpaste, scents or additions of any kind, and no sex. In addition to the deep inner purification, other plants are used for daily plant baths to physically and energetically wash away the toxins and energies that are released in the process.

All of these restrictions enhance the cleansing process over the extended time of the *dieta*, which dates back to prehistory. As time passes subjects lose their telltale human scents, particularly pheromones, hormones, and other secretions that jaguars and other animals with a highly refined sense of smell can detect, making the hunters virtually invisible to them and their primary sensory modalities. The constant refined ingestions and plant baths result in the subject not only smelling like the jungle, but they *become* the jungle, giving them a distinct hunting advantage.

These intense practices fine tune the subject's own senses bringing great clarity and a highly refined perception of their immediate reality, further adding to their hunting advantage. Aside from the intensified state of awareness that comes from this extreme purification which historically prepared them for hunts, battles, or other challenges, their conscious awareness of their field of perception expands at inner and outer levels making them psychologically and mentally clear for the task at hand.

These hard won physical and perceptual enhancements bring deep inner shifts from the resonance that comes from being sympathetic to and in sync with the plant spirits and the energies they manifest. One of the intriguing results of this immersion into what shamans characterize as the spirit world is the agreed upon encompassing energetic field that opens up the ability to not only commune with the plants and the distinctive energies of their unique spirits and personalities, but also to the distinctive energies and personalities of the animal kingdom.

This phenomenon is reinforced by widespread reports from Ayahuasca drinkers of directly experiencing and communing with or being "possessed" by specific animal energies that are common to the Ayahuasca experience, regardless of whether they are in the jungle or in a major North American city.

Among the numerous totems claimed by participants, or which they say actually choose them, the most common are condors, jaguars, and snakes which have a deeper meaning going all the way back to prehistoric cultures. Those experiencing these energies or spirits often roar and growl through no volition of their own like jaguars, flap their legs like wings, or feel their bodies swaying seemingly of its own accord to distinctive serpentine movements. Other animals and insects like hummingbirds, butterflies, dragonflies, dolphins, and other aquatic totems can play big parts as well.

This phenomenon with its roars, "wing flapping" and other indicators that an animal spirit is present or "possessing" its host forms the core of shape shifting mythologies where shamans reportedly have the ability to change their form into that of their familiar animal totems.

In this way shamans share the distinct, intimate resonant vibration of these entities in the same energetic way they do with the morphogenetic field of plants, becoming one with them by sharing the same frequency. In the same way they have to surrender to the plant teachers to discover what mysteries may be revealed, shamans must humble themselves to their animal familiars as the conductor transmitters of their experience.

In the lore of the jungle, by sharing in the vibratory field of the animal's spirit energy, in a state of surrender on that entity's terms, that animal learns from the human by seeing things through human eyes while the human learns other modes of perception from seeing things through the animal's eyes.

In this manner, by mutual agreement and the understanding that comes from sympathetically sharing the same energetic field and perception of specific animals, combined with the invisibility that comes from the physical purifications that makes the hunters virtually invisible to the primary sensory modalities of their prey, the shaman hunts the animals in spirit first, then follows through what has happened in the spirit world in the physical world in the actual physical hunt, aided by his cultivated invisibility.

This learned ability of shamans to tune in to and commune with these diverse plant and animal energies that we all share the world with allows them to experience them in a direct, definitive, and subjective manner that helps them understand other perspectives. This cultivates empathy which is the ability to understand and share the feelings of another, and opens them up in ways that only direct experience can, while aiding them in developing the critical skills necessary for what is defined as soul retrieval.

FINDING OUR WAY HOME

As discussed earlier, by paying attention we can cultivate witness consciousness and discover the meaning of the expression, "Where your attention goes, there your energy goes," which comes from our self-created focal point that is responsible for our thoughts and actions. Simply by paying attention and observing, we enhance presence and mindfulness while not allowing our sense of well-being to rely on anything other than our own presence of awareness.

When we are focused and tuned-in in this manner, our unique witness consciousness acts as a sympathetic and empathic transmitter, taking the role of "conductor" to get our orchestra of thoughts, feelings, emotions, and perceptions to "sing the same tune". Instead of denying uncomfortable feelings and perceptions that create a non-harmonious asynchronous state, what if we sought out and embraced them?

Among their many definitions, shamans are called bridges because of their ability to travel to other realms to retrieve healing knowledge and recover lost souls in what is called soul retrieval. They are also referred to as wounded healers, because in discovering and healing the source of their own traumas and injuries, they gain the ability to recognize and heal those same wounds in others.

When we are egocentric, our shadow aspects see our shortcomings in others and projects them onto them, judging and magnifying them in order to avoid seeing those very same things in itself. This survival mechanism is a protective strategy to keep it autonomous and separated because it fears losing its very existence, and in this process it keeps us self-centered and wrapped up in a bubble of egocentricity.

When a shaman through hard work and discomfort raises their awareness and gets past the mortal terror this invokes, they discover the hidden wounds within themselves and become sympathetic and empathic to those traumas. Instead of denying these wounds that they themselves have created, they embrace them like the abandoned aspects or sub-personalities that they are, and "bring them home".

In discovering the origins of their trauma induced creations, embracing them and taking responsibility, this process brings a shift from being reactive and unconsciously ego or personality driven, to being conscious and actively essence driven. By discovering the source of their own hidden pain discovered through the soul retrieval of their own subpersonalities, shamans receive the gift of compassion which allows them to heal those very same wounds in others through their recognition and acceptance of that which they found within themselves.

Gurdjieff taught that man consists of two parts: *essence* and *personality*. Essence in man is what is *his own*. Personality in man is what is "not his own". "Not his own" means what has come from outside, what he has learned, or reflects, which includes all traces of exterior impressions left in the memory and in the sensations, all words and movements that have been learned and all feelings created by imitation.

All this is "not his own", all this is personality which is created partly by the intentional influences of other people, and partly by involuntary imitation of them when a child itself. In the creation of personality a great part is also played by "resistance" to people around them and by attempts to conceal from them something that is their own.

In Gurdjieff's words:

"Essence is the truth in man; personality is the false. But in proportion as personality grows, essence manifests itself more and more rarely and more and more feebly and it very often happens that essence stops in its growth at a very early age and grows no further. It happens very often that the essence of a grown up man, even that of a very intellectual and, in the accepted meaning of the word, highly 'educated' man, stops on the level of a child of five or six. This means that everything we see in this man is in reality 'not his own'. What is his own in man, that is, his essence, is usually only manifested in his instincts and

in his simplest emotions. There are cases, however, when a man's essence grows in parallel with his personality. Such cases represent very rare exceptions especially in the circumstances of cultured life. Essence has more chances of development in men who live near to nature in difficult conditions of constant struggle and danger."

Psychology has historically dismissed shamans as schizophrenics, epileptics, and hysterics. Jung stated that shamanism works out of a primitive mentality that sees the psyche as outside the body, whereas modern culture views the psyche as inside. What separates shamanism and psychotherapy is a clash of metaphysics.

Mainstream psychotherapy locates the real "inside" and constructs a topography of drives, instincts, archetypes, complexes and the like to explain our experience as the result of interior dynamics, while shamanism locates the real "outside" and maps a greater cosmos comprised of a Lower World, Middle World, Upper World, and the entities that live in them.

What if the solution to this paradox were to lie hidden at its center where both sides of this dichotomy co-existed? What if deep inside your inner landscape you found an energetic portal that brought you further out into realms and dimensions you could never have imagined?

Aside from the fact that in Ayahuasca shamanism it is often the healer who takes the medicine, one of the fascinating things about it and the effects of its psychoactive component DMT is the agreed upon psychological landscape, replete with crystal castles, plant, animal, and other spirits, and their places in the lower, middle, and upper worlds, regardless of the time and geographic location of the experience. Being agreed upon by those bold or lucky enough to brave its frontiers makes it a consensual reality, but where would you locate this "place"?

In many ways we experience our psyches as "outside." Using our dreams as an example, if they were strictly internal, they would take us wandering around inside the organs and tissues of our own bodies, but they do not. They take us to tropical islands, strange nether worlds, and the sky as well as many other places into waking consciousness.

From our subjective experience of them our dreams are "out there" in the cosmos of dreaming. If we remain faithful to our experience the way indigenous societies do, we have to say that the unconscious of our dreaming sojourns are not invisible realms inside our heads, hearts, or stomachs. The domains that we travel through in our dreams and shamanic journeys are experienced as an alternate cosmos with a different set of rules, invisible to our ordinary awareness of space and time while suffusing and extending it far beyond in infinite directions.

If we try to give an account of a nonrational experience that attempts to describe things the way we experienced them, for example shamanic journeys that take place in the unconscious, what we mean is that we travel through a realm that is unknown to ordinary awareness, one that does not take place in the space and time of our everyday experience of consensual reality. It takes place in an *imaginal cosmos* no less real than this one, but radically different.

Furthermore, like the hypothesis of the unconscious, the shamanic realm of imaginal sojourns is in a sense *more real* than that of everyday awareness, making psychology's definition of the unconscious the greater reality within which our ordinary awareness is too fragmentary and narrow to adequately understand itself. Here, the shamanic point of view is in agreement, for shamanism finds that everyday events have a larger meaning that can only be appreciated when we journey out of the everyday into the greater cosmos that encompasses this little one, so the forces of the shamanic cosmos shape and determine what happens to us in our everyday lives.

Jung described "soul loss" as a drop in the level of mental functioning, characterized by depression, uncertainty, inattention, powerlessness, and the like, saying that a quantity of psychic energy which normally belongs to the ego has disappeared into the unconscious. From an energetic perspective, this is described as an energy leak. This lost package of libido would normally power our daily activities with attentiveness, enthusiasm, and decision-making.

According to Jung, a psychological cure would entail recovering this lost energy by descending into the unconscious through dreams, visions, and active imagination to find out what that energy is up to as the energy lost from consciousness does not cease to exist. It's up to something, stirring up imaginal adventures in that other world. By participating in those adventures and discovering their emotional and symbolic significance for everyday life, the energy leak can be repaired and restored so that life can resume with new vigor and follow a more satisfying direction. In this context, this lost sense of self can be found in that alternate cosmos that interpenetrates and extends beyond this one.

From the point of view of psychology, shamanism works with the metaphysical assumption that the soul or quantum of psychic energy that has been lost is a distinct, recognizable entity that can be found and recovered. The errant soul or sub-personality is lost, not simply in a dark corner of our personal dreamscape, but in an objective realm that is accessible to anyone who knows how to enter it.

This shamanic perspective goes far beyond the psychological, but its success demonstrates its accuracy. Shamanism and psychology may be suspicious of one another because to psychology, these shamanic events appear to be based on a kind of hocus-pocus occultism, while shamanism perceives that mere psychology is barred by its own dualistic and word-oriented assumptions from gaining access to a realm of experience that is real, but generally unknown to our Western consensus.

As Jung's thought matured his psychology became more and more shamanic, at first characterized by his discovery of what he called the feeling-toned complex stemming from trauma that established a complex of powerlessness and defeat, leaving a fragment or sub-personality that interpreted the world as a hostile and overpowering place. This worldview worked unconsciously over the course of months and years, collecting more and more evidence of its misleading accuracy.

The way to get free of such a complex is not to take it on directly and demonstrate its inaccuracy in an intellectual manner, but to *replace* it with another more functional and emotionally compelling complex. In other words, the solution lies in giving this sub-personality a new job by giving it another worldview that is already implicit, but undiscovered. Its superiority will be self-evident, and it will impart a feeling-tone of greater self-confidence.

Jung's search for a more powerful complex led him deeper into the psyche and to the discovery of what he called archetypes -- universal human themes, modes of perception, and patterns of behavior invested with compelling emotional values that draw the subject into a new way of life by sending them into an archetypal dreamscape to discover what their lost libido was up to in the domain of mythological images.

Here there is an agreement with shamanism that there is a greater cosmos accessible to imaginative faculties that are neglected in everyday waking consciousness. In *Symbols of Transformation,* Jung accepted the proposition that this greater cosmos, the domain of the unconscious, is *objective* in the sense that it works to effect changes in people's lives and assist them in discovering their unconscious wholeness, recovering soul parts that have been split off. It is considered a *collective* realm shared by everyone. Shamanism shares a number of agreements with Jungian psychology, but the two disciplines go about their work in different ways.

MOM OR DAD:
THE ASEXUAL PARENT ANSWERS THE CALL

In *The Psychology of the Transference* Jung articulated a shamanic perspective where he describes therapist and patient as sharing a single soul between them that has the quality of a deceptive guide that embodies the native American archetype of coyote the trickster. Jung called this guide that shares virtually identical qualities with Mother Ayahuasca in Amazonian cultures Mercurius, a Hermes-like spirit that has the unitary perspective of the Holy Ghost of Christianity and the destructive and fragmentary quality of the serpent of chaos. For purposes of this discussion Mother Ayahuasca and Mercurius can be considered one and the same spirit or intelligence, and the processes they engender are virtually identical.

In either case, the old habitual no longer functional worldview of the patient and the healer is broken up and destroyed by these instinctual forces of unintegrated archetypes. This demolition or ego death and rebirth, as painful and frightening as it always is, works in the service of a new integration under the guiding spirit of this god or goddess of transformation. This is the shamanic equivalent of the death and dismemberment hero's journey to the underworld popularized in mythology world wide.

In these sessions, Jung discusses holding himself open, vulnerable, and unprotected by his professional persona, unconcerned by the possibility that his "shadow may enter" the interaction with his patient, apparently believing that if the analysand feels cruelly treated, this is what the guiding spirit he referred to as "the Great Man" required.

The Great Man was neither Jung himself nor the patient, but a Third direction-giving "Presence," an autonomous Spirit that guided the process. Sometimes the Great Man was conceived as an unconscious factor within Jung himself that he listened to. At other times the Great Man was understood to be the patient's soul or potential wholeness he was addressing, but more often than not, the Great Man was experienced as a Third Partner who was neither in Jung's head, nor in the head of the patient, but *in the space between them both*. This space was described as the background against which they met and in dialogue with which they came to understand themselves in a new, more adequate manner where the world of habitual, everyday consciousness dissolves into whizzing molecules and the patient no longer knows who they are. Instead they have a sense that neither they nor Jung was directing the interaction; rather someone spoke through them, and someone, *not Jung*, spoke through him. Sometimes this altered state of consciousness was described as a Self-to-Self encounter, and sometimes as directed by a Third who was taken to be a two million year-old Man. It was an overwhelming experience which could result in elation, inflation, or a cruel belittlement which could be characterized as tough love. The patient often felt that their mind was being read and felt transparent, a subjective condition sometimes experienced as gratifying and sometimes as a dangerous descent into a perilous underworld.

The shamanic elements in Jung's analysis are unmistakable. He sets off on a monologue, not knowing where he is going, but following the guidance of the so-called Great Man, who seems to have all the characteristics of a Spirit Guide. In Jung's words, this being is not a conviction, not an assumption. It is a *Presence* and a *fact*. It *happens*.

Furthermore, the Great Man knows both the therapist and the patient better than they know themselves against the background of a greater, timeless cosmos, which is why he is described as being two million years old. Jung, in fact, *defined* analysis in the last decade of his life as an extended dialogue with the Great Man in which both therapist and patient come to know themselves within the context of the Great Man's wisdom. This larger perspective is what the patient needed to discover the wholeness of their soul. Jung discovered that his own identity was rearranged and enlarged suggesting an important reason why so many of the shamans described in Eliade's classic, *Shamanism, Archaic Techniques of Ecstasy*, need to shamanize. When they fail to practice their calling regularly, they fall sick because they lose their meaning-giving connection with that greater context, the cosmos through which they journey and the wisdom of their Spirit Guides.

An analysis guided by the Great Man, however, draws the patient into a trialogue with three parties actively contributing to the work: healer, patient, and Great Man. Jung's disciple from California, Jane Wheelwright, described the breakdown of the world where the domain of space and time flew apart into whizzing molecules and melting shapes. The realm of our public consensus -- what the modern West takes to be the only world there is; the reality we measure in feet, seconds, and degrees all blurs and becomes indistinct the moment the Great Man's voice is heard.

In trialogue with the Great Man, as in Ayahuasca sessions, healer and patient are drawn into an altered state of consciousness where the oneness of all things becomes more vivid than their separate identities and they find themselves in a perilous underworld of unfamiliar landmarks where the needle of their everyday compass spins uselessly. Certainty resides only in the Great Man, or mother who guides their interaction according to a cosmic wisdom they dimly intuit but cannot grasp.

When Jung said he listened within to speak whatever popped into his mind, he shifted his attention away from the sensory world to what he called the background where patient and analyst are carried along by a current of fascination and new topics flood harmoniously into the space between them. Lovers know this experience very well as they too are in touch with the background.

What Jung called the background, also known as the greater cosmos, is with us all the time, but we screen it out in ordinary states of consciousness and we are frightened of it for good reason. Imagine trying to negotiate our superhighways and crowded urban streets while open to such a strange underworld. The problem is that most of us screen it out too thoroughly, losing contact with the greater and deeper meaning of our existence. Even those of us relatively free of neurotic conflicts lose a good deal of our natural human spirituality, and those who have lost their souls have screened out so much that their lives become a disempowered misery. We have all lost our greater selves to some extent and screened out too much, losing a minimal sense of self that has been banished to the background dwelling in a place very much like the underworld of the myth of Orpheus and Eurydice.

In an analysis conducted by the Great Man, the errant soul is not rounded up and led back. Rather the patient travels into the greater cosmos along with their healer and *becomes* their soul, dropping their everyday obsession with impotence and survival to become united with their greater identity by making an imaginal journey guided by the Great Man or Mother into the background of their narrowly constructed life, vividly *living* in those minutes with the unforgettable power of their whole being until their soul has been restored.

Because shamanism takes the real as being outside the individual, it assumes that the soul has gotten lost -- strayed into a foreign realm -- and can only be retrieved by a specialist who has learned something of the topography of the greater cosmos and acquired a Spirit Guide to direct their search for a soul that has wandered far from its host. Meanwhile psychotherapy, because it takes the real as being inside the individual, assumes that the soul itself is not really lost and has not strayed, but rather is present but unrecognized. The patient has become unconscious of their soul's presence, but the soul doesn't have to be chased and led. The doors of perception have to be opened so the subject can consciously connect with a created soul or subpersonality that has been there all along.

Neither the shaman nor the therapist is capable of effecting the cure in ordinary consciousness. Both have to enter an altered state of awareness and open themselves to the guidance of a Third, a Spiritual Presence far wiser than they are. This Third Agent in the healing -- whether it is called *the* Great Man, *my* Spirit Guide, or Mother Ayahuasca has complete understanding of the human participants as well as the work they need to do. Both the shaman and the therapist find the soul through an imaginal journey under the guidance of that Third. Whether the healer travels through a cosmic dreamscape or relays stories concocted by the Guide, the shaman's journey itself can be seen as a concoction of the Guide. The important piece appears to be finding the soul which means acquiring a living experience of having a soul and being a soul.

A psychologist would want to know the mechanics of how the cure was effected and the inner dynamics that brought about these changes. An analysis conducted by the Great Man answers that the cure is effected by redirecting the patient's attention away from the narrow world of victimhood to the archetypal world where questions of ultimate meaning arise.

What is the meaning of death? What does it mean to live a life in which death is a certainty? The patient's attention is seduced away from the obsessions of their complex, and they begin to look at the cosmic picture. What they see there is so compelling that the tyranny of the complex is undermined and the cosmic realm of the background where their soul/subpersonality has been living unconsciously emerges to the forefront of their attention and generates a powerful fascination for their whole being, and the bars of their psychological prison have been sprung.

It seems self-evident that if a shaman is able to find and retrieve a soul, they must be in some kind of contact with that soul, and in its own way the soul must feel this connection as strongly as the shaman. If shamans are in general agreement that they do not effect the cure strictly by their own power, but rather through their Spirit Guides and Power Animals, something like a trialogue must be involved. In this regard, shamanism and an analysis conducted by the Great Man have a great deal in common and we are left with only one major difference between them, namely the explicitness of the trialogue structure. In an analysis directed by the Great Man, the trialogue occupies the foreground of consciousness for both analyst and patient, but in shamanism the trialogue structure lingers in the background. How do we account for this?

The most probable answer resides in the differences in the altered states of consciousness that come in an analytic cure as opposed to a shamanic one, which are respectively reverie and trance. For the definitions of these states, Dan Merkur's book, *Becoming Half Hidden: Shamanism and Initiation Among the Inuit* tells us that trance is characterized by a state of involuntary belief. While in the trance state we are incapable of doubting the truth and reality of the visions we encounter believing without *choosing* to believe. Doubts may occur to us after we return to an ordinary state of consciousness and recall the events of our trance, but during the trance itself, we can no more doubt the reality we experience in that state. Nagging doubts about the reality of the imaginal world we encounter in reverie can be suppressed, but they cannot be abolished, making reverie an altered state where we *voluntarily choose* to accept our visions as if they were as common as every day waking events.

Human consciousness is a fragile and limited thing and the fact that we all to a greater or lesser extent, lose our soul in everyday life dramatically illustrates this fragility. Shamans emphasize again and again the role of *trust* and *intent* in their work and when it comes to the work of finding and restoring souls, we have to work within our human limitations and can only be conscious of so much in any given moment. Shamanism and psychotherapy have much to learn from one another and the place to begin is with the experience of taking direction from Spirit or essence whether it is characterized as a Great Man or a Great Mother as opposed to being subject to the whims of our competing sub-personalities.

ARE THE INMATES RUNNING THE ASYLUM?

The Stranger was singer-songwriter Billy Joel's fifth studio album, and it remains his best-selling non-compilation album, ranked number 70 on Rolling Stone's list of the 500 greatest albums of all time. In the opening lines of the title track of the same name Joel tells us that, "We all have a face that we hide away forever and we take them out and show ourselves when everyone has gone, some are satin, some are steel, some are silk, and some are leather, they're the faces of the stranger, but we love to try them on."

The Stranger is a brilliant ode to the human shadow and no doubt appealed to the collective attention of listeners on subconscious levels by the deep truths it contains. What faces do we conceal and what faces do we show to the world?

As discussed earlier, all that we deny about ourselves constitutes unconscious aspects of our personality that the conscious ego does not identify in itself because it is our "dark side". We typically reject or remain ignorant of these least desirable aspects of our personalities making our shadow largely negative, as it consists of everything that we are not fully conscious of, but there are positive aspects that remain hidden, especially in people with low self-esteem, anxieties, and false beliefs. To truly know ourselves we must accept our dark side and to deal with the dark sides of others we have to know our own.

According to Jung, the shadow, being instinctive and irrational, is prone to psychological projection where a perceived personal inferiority is recognized as a moral deficiency in someone else which results in insulating and harming individuals by acting as a thickening veil of illusion between the ego and the real world.

In reality we are a veritable "cast of thousands" that can change moods, perceptions, and outlooks, depending on which sub-personality is in charge, and this can change from moment to moment. If we observe closely, we can often see instantaneous changes in the facial expressions of people when their sub-personalities surface to take control, making them look like completely different people than the face they usually show to the world, particularly when they are stressed.

As far back as 1915 Gurdjieff characterized this phenomenon in a talk to his followers.

"One of man's important mistakes, one which must be remembered, is his allusion in regard to his I.

"Man such as we know him, the 'man machine', the man who cannot 'do', and with whom and through whom everything 'happens', cannot have a permanent and single I. His I changes as quickly as his thoughts, feelings, and moods, and he makes a profound mistake in considering himself always one in the same person; in reality he is *always a different person*, and not the one he was a moment ago.

"*Man has no permanent and changeable I.* Every thought, every mood, every desire, every sensation, says I. And then each case it seems to be taken for granted that this I belong to the *Whole*, to the whole man, and that a thought, a desire, or an aversion is expressed by this Whole. In actual fact there is no foundation whatever for this assumption. Man's every thought and desire appears and lives quite separately and independently of the Whole. And the Whole never expresses itself, for the simple reason that it exists, as such, only physically as a thing, and in the abstract as a concept. Man has no individual I. But there are, instead, hundreds and thousands of separate small I's, very often entirely unknown to one another, never coming into contact, or, on the contrary, hostile to each other, mutually exclusive and incompatible. Each minute, each moment, man is saying or thinking 'I'. And each time his I is different. Just now it was a thought, now it is a desire, now a sensation, now another thought, and so on, endlessly. *Man is a plurality*. Man's name is legion.

"The alteration of I's, their continual obvious struggle for

supremacy, is controlled by accidental external influences. Warmth, sunshine, fine weather, immediately call up a whole group of I's. Cold, fog, rain, call up another group of I's, other associations, other feelings, other actions. There is nothing in man able to control this change of I's, chiefly because man does not notice, or know of it; he lives always in the last I."

We learn our coping strategies by observing and mirroring the behaviors of those around us, which is why Gurdjieff said that we are "controlled by accidental external influences", especially when dealing with traumatic situations, and though those deeply embedded behaviors were learned by our subpersonalities in the same manner, this does not make them correct responses. More often than not, these learned responses are replete with errors of interpretation and reaction that may temporarily defuse the trauma happening in the moment at hand, but do not solve the actual problem in the long run. Ultimately these responses are delegated to the depths of shadow in the form of sub-personalities which become trauma induced stock responses that act as a protective mechanism of illusion between the ego and the real world.

The important point to grasp here is that *we are the creators of these traumatized entities that fill our inner personal universe and are reflected by those outside of us*, especially when we project them outside of us and deny their existence within us, essentially abandoning our own creations.

When we meet people for the first time, we seek out what are referred to as "attention points", things we have in common with them like sports, music, the arts, or anything else we might have in common where we can connect with mutual interest. In this manner we pave the way to sharing similar thoughts, or to put it in other terms, we seek resonance with that person by sharing common vibrations as a place and energy to bond. This whole phenomenon is especially prevalent in today's tribal rave and festival culture where large groups of people bond in a loving vibration, often enhanced by drugs like MDMA which is an empathogen, a class of psychoactive drugs that produce experiences of emotional communion, oneness, relatedness, empathy, and sympathy. This experience bonds them in the shared medium of the music and the tribal beats, enveloping them in an all around "feel good vibe".

What we don't realize in our bonding and meeting of people is that the subconscious elements of our shadow also draws them to us through its familiarity and recognition of their shadow aspects.

When we find ourselves swallowed up in negative emotions, they tend to overwhelm and blind us to the truth of the situation through judgment, projection, denial, and other egoic survival strategies, but if we can "wake up" to the illusion and raise our awareness to the point of having a greater presence of mind we can ask important questions of our reactions.

What is the quality of this emotional energy and how does it make us feel?

Whose eyes are we seeing it through?

What mask are we wearing?

What filters have we taken on?

All of this interconnectedness and interaction reinforces the notion that we are all one, connected in our hearts, minds, and spirits. Shamans believe that everything is interconnected, including man, plants, animals, trees, and for that matter every part of creation. American Indians often refer to these other beings as brothers.

On an esoteric level, everything is connected within everything else in what modern physicists call a holographic manner. To record a hologram, a coherent light beam passes through a beam splitter. Some of the light scattered from an object or a set of objects falls on the recording medium. The other part of the split beam reflects off of a mirror. This second light beam is known as the reference beam, which also illuminates the recording medium, so that interference occurs between the two beams. The resulting light field generates a seemingly random pattern of varying intensity, which is recorded in the hologram.

An interesting property of holograms is that if one is cut up into smaller pieces, each portion contains information about the whole object.

If you look at the Internet with this paradigm in mind you will realize that the World Wide Web is really a huge mirror of the collective consciousness of humanity. All of the information is contained everywhere in the whole and much of this information is not accurate; it comes from someone's reflection on something which is often distorted and biased either unconsciously or intentionally.

An interesting property of mirrors is that they often show us what we do not want to see and if the mirror is distorted, so is the reflection.

In World War II before television, those outside of the war zone got their information from newspapers, radios, and newsreels, all of which were filtered through the individual viewpoints of reporters, their editors, and government censors. The Vietnam War has been called the first televised war, but even these images were filtered through a few major networks censored by their editors and the government.

In the new age of the 21st century we have Internet access with technological mirrors known as digital cameras, cell phones, and all manner of instantaneous communication. Because of these mirrors the editors and the censors are being bypassed and the mirror of truth is laying bare the lies of governments and the atrocities of war as well as the lies and propaganda of diverse agendas.

Everyone is buzzing about the latest scandals, not to mention the numerous incidents of police brutality, racial conflicts, mass murders, political corruption and more. The list is endless. The phenomena of Facebook allowed Egyptians to plan out and execute a relatively nonviolent overthrow of an oppressive government, and the violence that did occur was instantly transmitted out to the World Wide Web for the entire world to see.

Literally on another front, many believe that our erratic weather patterns, floods, wildfires, and earthquakes are a reflection of the turbulence going on within human consciousness, and many believe that this turbulence is the chaos that precedes the birth of something new.

If you do acknowledge that we are all connected as one, then each of us is a mirror to each other in a holographic manner from the macrocosm of the collective, down to the microcosm of our individual selves, down to the sub-personalities that make up what we think of as "I", but is in fact many. Some of our sub-personalities we like and we constantly take them out and show them to the world. Others we don't like and we repress them, making them our shadow which we don't want to acknowledge.

Mirrors often show us what we do not want to see. If you have the ability and the strength to be honest with yourself, and you desire to be a whole integrated person, then the work lies in reintegrating your hidden shadow(s). They aren't called your shadow for nothing. They are cunning, elusive, and some would rather see the death of you than be found out. They think that if they are discovered that they will die, which contains a grain of truth because in order to be reborn, a death is necessary.

Most of us deny our shadows and the trick that the shadow plays is to project itself onto others trapping us in self-righteousness and judgment so that the waters are muddied, distorting the reflection from our mirror. This is the key. If you can bear the reflection you can gradually come to realize that what you strongly dislike and often hate in others creates strong emotional reactions, because it is a reflection of that which you do not want to acknowledge or take responsibility for inside of you. It takes great courage to look at your self in the glare of this mirror and admit this.

Take a good look at everyone in your life. Some of them are drawn to and support your darker unconscious nature, and some are drawn to and reflect your lighter more conscious side. Some of their sub-personalities are drawn to both the light and dark aspects of your many selves.

If you believe that we are all one then the mirrors are there reflecting back from everywhere that you look. Any time you feel self-righteous, judgmental, and superior, you can be sure that you are seeing your shadow being reflected back to you.

Once you discover, acknowledge, and embrace these abandoned, infantile ego creations with compassion, don't "kill them", which is a popular modern day pop culture spiritual admonition. Give them a new job. You created them and in spite of their misguided actions they are trying to protect you at all costs. You reside at the center of their universe so take a good look at who is in your life and what feelings they engender in you.

SHAMANIC MIRRORING AND THE WIZARD OF OZ

The people in our lives mirror our different aspects and sub-personalities, providing us with reflections of our inner world and the outer world is a reflection of the inner, much of which is shadow, good and bad. Some of the reflections can be beautiful, but many are undesirable and denied. This circular diagram from Robert McKee's ***Story*** provides an excellent map of the zones and levels of personal conflict we can experience. Any zone can interact with any other zone in any number of ways, providing ample opportunity to discover the complexity of our inner and outer relationships.

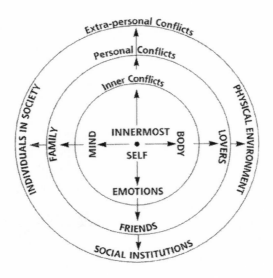

You can also envision this as the "center of the universe" as it maps the interplay of energetic interactions that start in the middle and work their way out. At the center of the universe we find the innermost self which is composed of mind, body, and emotions. Everyone knows what it is like to have conflict between these three forces. Typically, one of them leads while the other two are relegated to shadow until a strong stimulus causes them to pop out -- sometimes when least expected.

Often when confronted with something we react in the following order; first with our intellect (mind), because that is what we have grown to depend on, then we might act by doing something (body), then we may feel good or bad about what we have done (emotion).

A woman might react with her feelings first (emotion), then think about how she reacted (mind), then do something (body).

Anyone, male or female can act in any combination of ways, but more often than not they lead with their strongest most habitual response at the expense of the other two.

What would it be like if someone reacted with all three simultaneously in a balanced way?

This is one of the goals of integrating the shadow in the process of individuation, and subsequently one of the rewards of personal power a shaman gets from getting dismembered or swallowed by the jaguar.

These three primary inner energies have been characterized throughout myth and history in many ways. The thinking mind is referred to as knowledge and wisdom, the moving body is referred to as energy and power, while the feeling of emotion is referred to as love. On one end of the spectrum the modern divide and conquer scientific mind set has given mind the most attention. Energetically it is the most stable. On the other end, emotion is the quickest, most mercurial, and hardest to control. The body usually serves the other two, though it holds deep wisdom of its own that is often ignored.

The Inca view of reality is a shamanic one that has three worlds; the upper world, represented by the condor, which has a rose color and is thought of as love (emotion). The middle world is represented by the jaguar or puma, and has an electric blue color signifying power (body). The lower world is represented by the serpent which has a gold color, signifying wisdom. When the three are combined in harmony and unity, they are believed to create a beautiful electric violet hue.

It is interesting to note the ways these three energies have been depicted in stories, particularly when we take into account how secondary characters mirror the inner life of the protagonist. One of the most striking examples of this is in **The Wizard of Oz** where we have Dorothy on her hero's quest to find her way home. Her three primary allies are the tin man, who wants a heart (love - emotion), the cowardly lion, who wants courage (power - body), and the scarecrow, who wants a brain (wisdom - mind).

Shamans navigate multiple realities because they realize that their power lies in how they filter, see, and react to the realms that they come in contact with by manipulating their perception with the knowledge that all they encounter comes to them through their own subjective experience.

In shamanism everything is connected to everything else. Plants, animals, man, and elemental spirits all interact and affect each other in visible and invisible ways. Shamans more than anyone else know that even though the center of the universe is right between their eyes, their real home is where the heart is.

THE HEART OF THE MATTER

The Temple of Anthropocosmic Man at Luxor is a masterpiece of art, science, and spirituality laid out in an elegant structure that is architecturally rendered to exhibit within its design and artwork the same proportions as the proportions of Man, as well as the mathematical and geometrical structure of the Cosmos and its locale within human consciousness. Pharaonic Consciousness not only recognized Man as the center of the Universe, it could formally equate it as well.

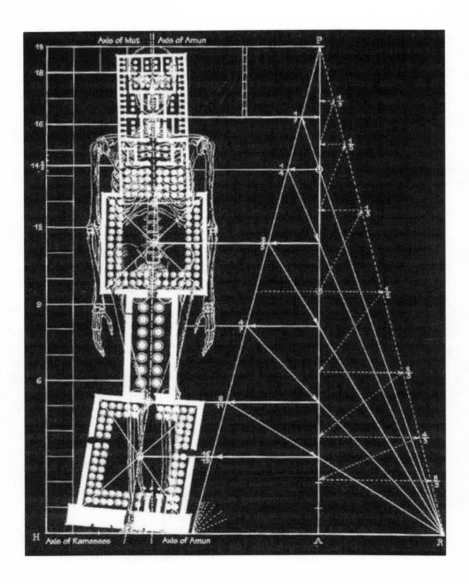

The Temple of Anthropocosmic Man

Gurdjieff had a similar interpretation.

"There is no need to study or investigate the sun in order to discover the matter of the solar world: this matter exists in ourselves and is the result of the division of our atoms. In the same way we have in us the matter of all other worlds. Man is, in the full sense of the term, a 'miniature universe'; in him are all the matters of which the universe consists; the same forces, the same laws that govern the life of the universe, operate in him; therefore in studying man we can study the whole world, just as in studying the world we can study man."

Gurdjieff's teachings followed the same model as the Temple of Man, although his diagram is a little different and appears a little more expansive in that he included All Worlds and the Moon in what he called "The Ray of Creation", which he characterized as an octave that repeats at many levels and sub-levels, but the principle remains the same.

Gurdjieff's Ray of Creation

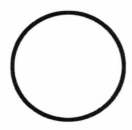

ABSOLUTE - 1 - Do

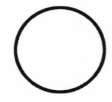

ALL WORLDS - 3 - Re

ALL SUNS - 6 - Mi

SUN - 12 - Fa

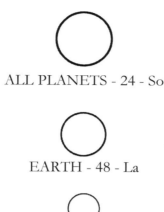

ALL PLANETS - 24 - So

EARTH - 48 - La

MOON - 96 - Ti

In Gurdjieff's model, the Whole, One, or *All*, he called the 'Absolute' because including everything within itself it is not dependent upon anything, and is the 'world' for 'all worlds' where All forms one single Whole, infinite and indivisible as the primordial state of things out of which by division and differentiation arises the diversity of the phenomena observed by us. In the Absolute vibrations are the most rapid and matter is the least dense and in the descending ray of creation the dampening vibrations are slower and matter denser. Lower down on the ray matter is still more dense and vibrations correspondingly slower.

Gurdjieff stated that matter possessing characteristics of materiality comprehensible to us is divided into several states according to its density; solid, liquid, and gaseous. Further gradations of matter are radiant energy like electricity, light, magnetism, and so on.

He referred to this octave as the table of hydrogen that served to determine the density of matter and the speed of vibrations, as well as the degree of intelligence and consciousness, because the degree of consciousness corresponded to the degree of density or the speed of vibrations. This means that the denser the matter, the less conscious and the less intelligent, and the denser the vibrations, the more conscious and the more intelligent.

The chain of worlds, the length of which are the Absolute forms the "ray of creation" which for us is the "world" in the widest sense of the term. The Absolute gives birth to a number, perhaps to an infinite number, of different worlds, each of which begins a new and separate ray of creation. The number of forces in each world, 1, 3, 6, 12, and so on, indicate the number of laws to which the given world is subject. The fewer laws that are in a given world, the nearer it is to the will of the Absolute, and the more laws there are in a given world, the further it is from the will of the Absolute.

Gurdjieff taught that we live in a world subject to forty-eight orders of laws, that is to say, very far from the will of the Absolute and in a very remote and dark corner of the universe. The ray of creation from world 1 down to world 96 indicate the number of forces, or orders of laws that govern the worlds in question. In the Absolute there is only one force and only one law - the single and independent will of the Absolute. In the next world there are three forces or three orders of laws, in the next six orders of laws, in the following one, twelve, etc. According to Gurdjieff, the earth has forty-eight orders of laws that we are subject to. If we lived on the moon we would be subject to ninety-six orders of laws and would not have the possibilities of escape that we now have.

Following this octave model of increasing densities of matter and creation, as well as intelligence, Gurdjieff defined the end of the ray, saying, "The souls that go to the moon, possessing perhaps even a certain amount of consciousness and memory, find themselves there under ninety-six laws, in the conditions of mineral life, or to put it differently, in conditions from which there is no escape apart from a general evolution in immeasurably long planetary cycles. The Moon is 'at the extremity', at the end of the world; it is the 'outer darkness' of the Christian doctrine 'where there will be weeping and gnashing of teeth'."

This ancient depiction of a holographic world view in which the microcosm is in the macrocosm so clearly demonstrated in the Temple of Anthropocosmic Man and in Gurdjieff's diagram is a shamanic belief that infuses the shaman's transformation and subsequently the ancient archetype of The Hero's Journey. The design and layout of the temple and its mathematical meaning provide the framework for our inner and outer universe.

In this model, the heart which can be considered the giver of life, is located at the center of man. It gives life to and supports all the other organs surrounding it in the same way that the sun at the center of our solar system gives life to and supports all of the planets surrounding it. Each planet that orbits this solar furnace which is the crucible of the heart has historically been attributed with its own personality. Mars has been called "The God of War", Venus "The Goddess of Beauty and Love", and the others, each with their own unique attributes, or to put it another way, their own unique energies.

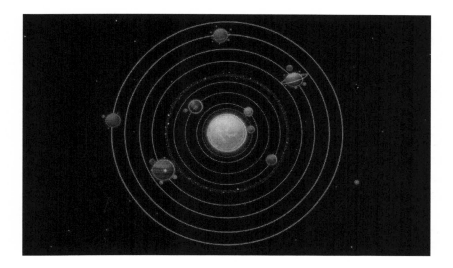

The Solar System

Centuries before it became a pop culture fad, Astrology was a highly respected science which was an integral part of Astronomy. In addition to the Earth and the seasonal signs of the zodiac, Astrology deals with ten planets, namely the Sun, the Moon (the two luminaries are considered planets in astrology), Mercury, Venus, Mars, Jupiter, Saturn, Uranus, Neptune, and Pluto. Each planet has its precise function in the natal chart, and represents a specific energy. The planet's action is influenced by the sign it tenants and plays out primarily in the area of life indicated by the house where it is posited.

In shamanism the heart in man is the sun of his personal cosmos which is connected to the sun, which is the giver of life in our solar system, especially on planet earth. This sun in turn is connected to a bigger sun, which is connected to a bigger sun, infinitely, essentially following Gurdjieff's ray of creation all the way back to Source.

Hafez, a 14th-century poet, best known for expressing the ecstasy of divine inspiration in the mystical form of love poems penned a wonderful verse that captures the essence of this belief.

Even After All this time The Sun never says to the Earth, "You owe me." Look What happens With a love like that, It lights the whole sky.

An old adage in shamanism made popular by Carlos Castaneda attributed to Don Juan, the Yaqui shaman, is that, "A warrior must follow a path with heart." In other words, follow your heart. If it takes you back to Source, then you have found your way home.

In the same way that the sun at the center of our solar system is influenced by and influences the planets in its orbit, so do the organs and their energies in the human body interact with its heart.

We are all at the heart of the universe that we are creating. Like the planets all of the people in our lives are energetic influences that represent different aspects of us that manifest different sides of our personalities. Our supporting allies mirror and support the good, including positive aspects of our shadow and the antagonistic ones reflect our darker side.

HOW WE CREATED THE
NON-SENSE PRISON WE LIVE IN

In the 21st century we find ourselves living in a paradoxical technological age where we are all connected with near instantaneous text and video communication as well as access to a vast storehouse of information both good and bad that spans the globe. In spite of this abundance of data, many of us spend our time alone on social media watching cat videos or some other silliness, or raising our blood pressure from divisive politics or some kind of social injustice. Not only are we more disconnected, isolated, and alienated from each other, evident in the way so many of us, even in social situations are glued to our smart phone screens, we are for the most part more divided and cut off from the natural world than ever before.

How could this happen?

The surprising answer to this quandary goes all the way back to how we originally altered our perception of reality in the way we chose to communicate.

The expressive, gestural basis of language was emphasized in the first half of the eighteenth Century by the Italian philosopher Giambattista Vico (1668 - 1744), who in his *New Science* wrote about how language arose from expressive gestures, suggesting that the earliest and most basic words took shape from expletives uttered in startled response to powerful natural events, or from the frightened, stuttering mimesis of such events - like the crack and rumble of thunder across the sky.

Shortly thereafter, in France, Jean-Jacques Rousseau (1712 - 1778) wrote about gestures and spontaneous expressions of feeling as the earliest forms of language, while in Germany, Johann Gottfried Herder (1744 - 1803) argued that language originated in our sensuous receptivity to the sounds and shapes of the natural environment.

In his embodied philosophy of language, Frenchman Maurice Merleau-Ponty (1908 - 1961) inherited this long-standing, somewhat heretical lineage. Linguistic meaning for him is rooted in the felt experience induced by specific sounds and sound-shapes as they echo and contrast with one another, each language a kind of song, a particular way of "singing the world."

Only if words are felt bodily presences like echoes or waterfalls, can we truly understand the power of a spoken language to influence, alter, and transform the perceptual world. To neglect this dimension and overlook the power that words have as spoken phrases to influence the body and modulate our sensory experience of the world around us is to render even the most mundane communicative capacity of language incomprehensible.

The innovation which gave rise to what became our alphabet was developed by Semitic scribes around 1500 B.C.E. and consisted of recognizing that almost every syllable of their language was composed of one or more silent consonantal elements, plus an element of sounded breath that we now call vowels. These silent consonants provided the bodily framework or shape that the sounded breath flowed through.

This original Semitic *aleph-beth* established a character or letter for each of the consonants while the sounded breath that the vowels added to the consonants were chosen by the interactive reader who varied the sounded breath according to the written context.

With the advent of the *aleph-beth*, a new distance opened up between human culture and the rest of nature. Pictographic and ideographic writing already involved a displacement of our sensory participation from the depths of the animate environment to the flat surface of our walls, clay tablets, or sheets of papyrus, but these written images typically related us back to the other animals in the environing earth. The pictographic glyph or character still referred to the animate phenomena of which it was the static image and it was that worldly phenomena that provoked from us the sound of its name.

The sensible phenomenon and its spoken name were still participant with one another in that the name remained an emanation of the sensible entity, but with a phonetic alphabet the written character no longer referred us to any sensible phenomenon out in the world, or to the name of such a phenomenon, but solely to a gesture made by the human mouth. This facilitated a concerted shift of attention away from any outward or worldly reference of the pictorial image, away from the sensible phenomenon that had previously called forth the spoken utterance, to the shape of the utterance itself, now invoked directly by the written character. A direct association was established between the pictorial sign and the vocal gesture, for the first time *totally bypassing the thing pictured*.

When we consider the early Semitic *aleph-beth*, we can recognize its pictographic inheritance. *Aleph*, the first letter is also the ancient Hebrew word for ox. The shape of the letter was an ox's head with horns turned over to become the letter A. Similarly, the name of the Semitic letter *mem* is the Hebrew word for water, which later became our letter M drawn as a series of waves. The letter *ayin*, which meant eye in Hebrew was drawn as a circle, the picture of an eye, which was made over into a vowel by the Greek scribes, eventually becoming our letter O and the Hebrew letter *qoph*. The Hebrew term for monkey was drawn as a circle intersected by a long dangling tail which gave us the letter Q.

With the transfer of phonetic writing to Greece, and the consequent transformation of the Semitic *aleph-beth* into the Greek alphabet, the progressive abstraction of linguistic meaning from the enveloping life-world reached a level of completion when the Greek scribes took on, with slight modifications both of shapes of the Semitic letters and their Semitic names. *Aleph*, the first letter which meant ox, became *alpha*, and *beth*, the second letter which meant house became beta, while *gimmel*, the third letter and the word for camel became gamma, and so on.

While the Semitic names had older non-grammatical meanings for those who spoke the Semitic tongue, the Greek version of those names had non-grammatical meaning for the Greeks. While they Semitic name for the letter was also the name of the sensorial entity commonly imagined by or associated with the letter, the Greek name had no sensorial reference whatsoever. While the Semitic name served as a reminder of the worldly origin of the letter, the Greek name served only to designate the human made letter itself. The pictorial iconic significance of many of the Semitic letters, which was memorialized in the spoken names was now lost.

Prior to the advent of the written word, oral traditions passed down through generations dating back to pre-history preserved the cultural knowledge of peoples. This practice is still in use today in many indigenous "illiterate" cultures. For the Greeks, the Homeric epics, probably written down in the seventh century B. C. E., are orally evolved poems that were sung and resung, shifting and complexifying long before they were written down and frozen in the form that we now know them in.

The Greek alphabet was adapted from the *aleph-beth* several centuries before Plato, most likely during the 8th Century B. C. E., but the new technology did not spread rapidly through Greece. It encountered resistance from a highly developed and ritualized oral culture. The traditions of pre-alphabetic Greeks lived in oral stories regularly recited and passed down from generation to generation by bards, or rhapsodes and the chanted tales carried within their nested narratives the accumulated knowledge of their culture.

Since they were not written down, they were never fixed, but shifted with each telling to fit the circumstances of a particular audience, gradually incorporating new practical knowledge while letting what was obsolete fall away. The sung stories along with the ceremonies they were linked with served as living encyclopedias of their culture, carrying and preserving the collected knowledge and customs of the community, and they themselves remained preserved through repetition and ritual reenactment so there was little need for reading and writing. According to literary historian Eric Havelock, for the first two or three centuries after its appearance in Greece, the alphabet was an interloper lacking social standing. It struggled to achieve use as the elite of society were all reciters and performers.

In a culture as thoroughly oral as the Greeks were back then, the alphabet could only take root by aligning itself with the oral tradition, so the first large written texts to appear in Greece, the *Iliad* and the *Odyssey* are paradoxically oral texts; not written compositions, but alphabetic transcriptions of orally chanted poems. Homer was an oral bard or rhapsode, from the Greek *rhapsoidein*, which meant to "stitch song together" which they did by "stitching together" an oral tapestry from a vast store of memorized epithets and formulaic phrases, embellishing and elaborating a cycle of stories that had already been improvised or "stitched together" by earlier bards since the Trojan War.

When the Homeric epics were recorded in writing, the art of the rhapsodes began losing their preservative and instructive function. The knowledge embedded in epic stories and myths was now captured for the first time in a visible fixed form which could be returned to, examined, and questioned. It was then, under the slowly spreading influence of alphabetic technology, that language began to separate itself from the animate flux of the world, becoming a ponderable presence in its own right.

In *The Muse Learns to Write*, Havelock stated, "It is only as language is written down that it becomes possible to think about it. The acoustic medium, being incapable of visualization, did not achieve recognition as a phenomenon wholly separable from the person who used it. But in the alphabetized document the medium became objectified. There it was, reproduced perfectly in the alphabet... No longer just a function of me the speaker, but a document with an independent existence."

The scribe or author could now dialogue with his own visible inscriptions, viewing and responding to his own words even as he wrote them down bringing a new power of reflexivity into existence, borne by the relation between the scribe and his scripted text.

Historically, Plato and his mostly non-literate teacher Socrates are recognized as the hinge on which the sensuous, mimetic, profoundly embodied style of consciousness proper to orality gave way to the more detached, abstract mode of thinking engendered by alphabetic literacy. It was Plato who carefully developed and brought to terms the collective thought structures appropriate to the new technology.

What this makes clear is that the shapes of our consciousness are shifting with the technologies that engage our senses much as we can now discern how the distinctive shape of Western philosophy was born at the meeting between the human senses and the alphabet in ancient Greece.

The invention of movable type by Johann Gutenberg in the fifteenth Century, and subsequently the printing press, in the dissemination of uniformly printed texts that it made possible ushered in the Enlightenment and the profoundly detached view of nature that prevails today in the modern world. In recent centuries the industrial and technological practice is made possible by this new distance from the natural world and have carried alphabetic awareness throughout the globe, infiltrating even those cultures that had retained iconic, idiographic writing systems.

Couple this with the modern day explosive growth of the internet and the proliferating disconnects we experience among ourselves and the natural world, and we see this distancing process exacerbated to a high degree of complexity.

LOST IN TRANSLATION

Many indigenous cultures worldwide, particularly the Apache of North America and the aborigines in Australia, which are the least technological of human cultures, we find the most intimate relationship between land and human language. In this context language is inseparable from song and story and songs and stories in turn, are inseparable from the shapes and features of the land. In these cultures the chanting of any part of a song cycle links the human singer to one of the animals or plants or powers within the landscape and binds the human singer to the land itself, to specific hills, rocks, and stream beds that are the visible correlate of those sung stanzas. Though generally directed more toward plants and animals, this is what Ayahuasca shamans do in ceremony when they play and sing icaros to these elemental spirits.

Given this interdependence between spoken stories and the sensible landscape, the ethnographic practice of writing down oral stories and disseminating them in published form forcibly tears them from the very "ground" of their being in the visible landforms and topographic features that materially embody and provoke them.

As the technology of writing spreads through a previously oral culture, the felt power and personality of particular places fades as the stories that express and embody that power are recorded in writing, rendering them separable from the actual places where the events in those stories occurred. The narrative can now be carried elsewhere and can be read in distant cities or on alien continents and soon become independent of any specific locale.

Previously, the power of spoken tales was rooted in the potency of the particular places where their events unfolded. While the recounting of certain stories might be provoked by specific social situations, their instructive value and moral efficacy was often dependent upon one's visible or sensible contact with the actual sites where those stories took place. In such cases contact with the regional landscape and the diverse sites or places within that landscape was not only the primary mnemonic trigger of the oral stories, it was integral to their preservation and to the culture itself.

Once stories are written down *the visual text became the primary mnemonic activator of the spoken stories.* The ink traces left by the pen as it traversed the page replaced the earthly actions left by the animals and ancestors in their interactions with the local land. The places themselves were no longer necessary to the remembrance of the stories and often became incidental to the tales. This arbitrary backdrop for human events might just as easily have happened elsewhere. The trans-human, ecological determinants of the original oral stories were no longer emphasized and often written out of the tales entirely.

In this manner stories and myths lost their oral performative character and forfeited their intimate links to the more than human earth as the land itself, stripped of the specific stories that once sprouted from every cave, streambed, and cluster of trees lost its multiplicitous power.

Human senses intercepted by the written word are no longer gripped and fascinated by the expressive shapes and sounds of particular places, and the spirits fall silent until the felt primacy of place is forgotten, superseded by a new, abstract notion of "space" as a homogeneous and placeless void.

The new concentration of humanity within permanent towns and cities and the increased dependence on the regulation and manipulation of spontaneous natural processes intensifies the growing estrangement of the human senses from the wild animate diversity where those senses evolved, which is directly related to the influence of writing upon human senses and our direct sensorial experience of the Earth around us.

Alphabetic writing undermined the embedded, place specific character of oral cultures in two distinct ways, one basically perceptual, the other primarily linguistic. Reading and writing entail highly concentrated forms of participation that displace the older participation between the human senses and the earthly terrain, essentially freeing human intention from the direct dictates of the land. Writing down the ancestral stories disengages them from particular places. This double retreat of the senses into spoken stories from the diverse places that once gripped them cleared the way for the notion of a pure and featureless space, an abstract concept that today has come to appear more primordial and real than the earthly places that we remain corporeally embedded in.

In order to read phonetically we have to disengage the synesthetic participation between our senses and the encompassing earth. The letters of the alphabet, each referring to a particular sound or sound gesture of the human mouth, function as mirrors that reflect us back upon ourselves establishing a new reflexivity between the human organism and its own signs, effectively short-circuiting the sensory reciprocity between that organism and the land. As mentioned earlier, this distancing phenomenon has been amplified and exacerbated exponentially in modern technological times through the impact of the internet. This new reflective intellect is the reflexive loop between ourselves and our written signs, making human encounters and events interesting in their own right, independent of their relation to natural cycles.

For the Apaches and other indigenous cultures like the aborigines, different paths through present terrains resonate with different stories from the Dreamtime, and every water hole, forest, and cluster of boulders or creek bed has its own dreaming and implicit life. The vitality of each place is rejuvenated by the human enactment, and en-*chant*-ment, of the storied events that crouch within it, making Dreamtime integral to the special surroundings.

The Hebrews are the first truly alphabetic culture that we know of, the first "people of the book". At the founding event of the Jewish nation atop Mount Sinai, Moses inscribed the commandments dictated by YHWH, the most sacred of God's names upon two stone tablets, presumably in an alphabetic script. Scholars place the exodus from Egypt around 1250 B.C.E., right at the time that the 22 letter consonantal *aleph-beth* was coming in to use in the area of Canaan or Palestine.

While the visible landscape provides oral tribal cultures with a necessary mnemonic or memory trigger for remembering ancestral stories, alphabetic writing enabled Hebrew tribes to preserve their cultural stories intact, even when the people were cut off for many generations from the actual lands where those stories took place. By carrying on its lettered surface the vital stories earlier carried by the terrain itself, the written text essentially became a portable homeland for the Hebrew people, and it is only by virtue of this portable ground that the Jewish people have been able to preserve their culture and themselves while in an almost perpetual state of exile from the actual lands where their ancestral stories unfolded. Many of the written narratives in the Bible are stories of this displacement and exile.

The most ancient stratum of the Hebrew Bible is structured by the motif of exile starting with the expulsion of Adam and Eve from the garden of Eden, to the long wandering of the Israelites in the desert. The Jewish sense of exile was never just a state of separation from a specific locale, it was and is also a sense of separation from the very possibility of being placed, from the very possibility of being entirely at home. This deeper sense of displacement, the sense of already being an exile is inseparable from alphabetic literacy, the great and difficult magic that the Hebrews were the first real caretakers of.

The burning alive of tens of thousands of women, most of them herbalists and midwives from peasant backgrounds, as "witches" during the sixteenth and seventeenth centuries may usefully be understood as the attempted, and nearly successful, extermination of the last orally preserved traditions of Europe - the last traditions rooted in the direct, participatory experience of plants, animals, and elements in order to clear the way for the dominion of alphabetic reason over a natural world increasingly construed as a passive and mechanical set of objects.

THE ANSWER IS BLOWING IN THE WIND

Elemental spirits are universally revered in shamanistic cultures and one of the most respected among them is the Wind, an invisible force that can be harnessed as well as storm out of control, leaving death and destruction in its wake. The fact that it is capable of delivering so much power, yet has no substance, defines it as not only a direct link to spirit, but spirit itself; formless, invisible, energy. If we remain still, we have no perception of air when it is at rest and we perceive and characterize it as *nothing* as it registers nothing with any of our senses, making it a perceptual enigma.

Air is the most pervasive presence we know. It surrounds and caresses us both inside and out, moving across our skin, between our fingers, around our arms and thighs, sliding along the roof of our mouths and down our throats to fill our lungs to feed our blood, which keeps us alive.

We cannot speak, act, or think without the participation of this fluid element and we exist in its depths the same way fish live immersed in the ocean. We can feel it moving against us and often taste, smell, and hear it as it swirls in our ears or moves through whispering leaves, or when it changes the shape, moves shifting clouds, or sends ripples along the surface of a lake. The fluttering feathers of a hummingbird, a spiraling leaf as it falls, and the slow drift of a seed through space indicate the presence of the air, yet we can never see the air itself.

This unseen enigma holds the mystery that enables life to live and unites our breathing bodies to the world around us and to the interior life of all that we perceive in the open field of this living presence, and what the plants breathe out, we and the animals breathe in, and what we breathe out plants breathe in. In shamanic thought, the air is the soul of the visible landscape that constitutes the secret realm where all beings draw their nourishment from. As the mystery of our living present, it is that most intimate absence felt as nothing where the present presences, providing a key to the forgotten presence of the earth.

Nothing is more common to the diverse indigenous cultures of the earth than a recognition of the air, wind, and breath as aspects of a singularly sacred power. By virtue of its pervasive presence, it's invisibility and its influence on all manner of visible phenomena, the air for oral people is the archetype of all that is ineffable, yet undeniably real and efficacious. Its obvious ties to speech in that spoken words are structured breath, and broken phrases take their communicative power from this invisible medium that moves between us lends the air a deep association with linguistic meaning and thought. Its ineffability is similar to the ineffability of awareness itself. Many indigenous people construe awareness or mind not as a power that resides inside their heads, but as a quality that they themselves are inside of along with the other animals, plants, mountains, and clouds.

In his book, *Holy Wind in Navajo Philosophy*, James Mikhail McNely asserts that the Navajo term *nilch'i,* meaning Wind, Air, or Atmosphere, suffuses all of nature and is that which grants life, movement, speech, and awareness to all beings. Additionally, the Holy Wind serves as the means of communication *between* all beings and elements of the animate world, making *nilch'i* central to the Navajo worldview.

For the Navajo *nilch'I* is a single unified phenomenon of the Wind in its totality comprised of many diverse aspects of partial Winds, each with their own name in the Navajo language. One of these - *nilch'i hwii'siziinii,* or the "Wind within one", refers to that part of the overall Wind that circulates within each individual. The Wind within one is in not autonomous, but a continual process of interchange with the various winds that surround us, and is a part of the Holy Wind itself.

When referring to the multiple Winds like Dawn Man, Dawn Woman, Sky Blue Woman, Twilight Man, Dark Wind, Wind's Child, Revolving Wind, Glassy Wind, Rolling Darkness Wind, and others, the Navajo are not speaking of abstract or ideal entities. These entities are not palpable phenomena like gusts, breezes, whirlwinds, eddies, storm fronts, cross currents, gales, whiffs, blasts, and breaths that they perceive in the fluid medium that surrounds and flows through their bodies.

The Navajo conviction that all of these subsidiary Winds are internal expressions of a single, inexhaustible mystery comes from the observation that the multiple vortices made by their own breathing, heat rising in waves, or the branches of trees as they sway in the surging air. All these currents and eddies swirling around and inside them are not entirely autonomous forces, but momentary articulations within the vast and fathomless body of Air itself.

For the Navajo the air in its capacity to provide awareness, thought, and speech has properties that European alphabetic civilization traditionally ascribe to an interior, individual human mind or psyche, yet by attributing these powers to the Air, and insisting that the "Winds within us" are continuous with the Wind at large, with the invisible medium that we are immersed in, Navajo elders suggest that what we call "mind" is not ours, and therefore not a human possession. Mind as Wind is a property of the encompassing world that humans and all other beings participate in. One's individual awareness and the sense of a personal self or psyche is simply that part of the enveloping Air that circulates within, through, and around one's body, so one's own intelligence is assumed from the start to be entirely participant with the swirling psyche of the land.

Our English term psyche and its modern offspring psychology, psychiatry, and psychotherapy are derived from the ancient Greek word *psyche*, which denoted not just the soul or the mind, but also breath or a gust of wind. The Greek noun was itself derived from the verb *psychein*, which meant to breathe or blow while another ancient Greek word for air, wind, and breath, *pneuma*, gives us pneumatic and pneumonia, while signifying that vital principle which in English we call "spirit".

The word spirit itself, despite all its incorporeal and non-sensuous connotations is directly related to the bodily term respiration through their common root in the Latin word *spiritus*, which meant breath and wind, as well as being the root of the words inspire and inspiration. Similarly the Latin word for soul, *anima* gives us animal, animation, animism, and unanimous, which is being of one mind or one soul. It also signified air and breath. These were not separate meanings. *Anima*, like *psyche*, originally named an elemental phenomenon that comprised both what we now call the air and what we now term the soul. The more specific Latin word *animus* signified that which thinks in us was derived from the same airy route, *anima*, itself derived from the older Greek term *anemos*, meaning wind.

We find an identical association of the mind with the wind and the breath in numerous ancient languages. Even an objective, scientifically respectable word as atmosphere displays its ancestral ties to the Sanskrit word *atman*, which signified soul as well as the air and the breath. A great many terms that refer to the air as a passive and insensate medium are derived from words that once identified the air with life and awareness. Words that now seem to designate a strictly immaterial mind or spirit are derived from terms that once named the breath as the very substance of that mystery.

For ancient cultures the air was a singular sacred presence. As the experiential source of both psyche and spirit, it appears as if that the air was once felt to be the very matter of awareness, the subtle body of the mind, and that awareness, far from being experienced as a quality that distinguishes humans from the rest of nature was felt as that which invisibly joined human beings to the other animals, plants, forests, and mountains as the unseen common medium of their existence.

Like so many other ancient tribal languages, Hebrew has a single word for both "spirit" and "wind", the word *ruach*, the spiritual wind, which is central to early Hebraic religiosity. Its primordiality and close association with the divine is evident in the first sentence of the Hebrew Bible:

When God began to create heaven and earth - the earth being unformed and void, with darkness over the surface of the deep and a wind (*ruach*) in God's sweeping over the water...

At the beginning of Hebrew creation, God is present as a wind moving over the waters, and breath, as we learn in the next section of Genesis, is the most intimate and elemental bond linking humans to the divine. It is that which flows most directly from God and man, for after God forms an earthling (*adam*) from the dust of the earth (*adamah*), he blows into the earthling's nostrils the breath of life, and the human awakens.

Although *ruach* refers to the breath, the Hebrew term used here is *neshamah* which denotes both the breath and the soul. While *ruach* generally refers to the wind or spirit at large, *neshamah* signifies the more personal, individual aspect of the wind, the wind or breath of a particular body like the "Wind within one" of the Navajo. In this sense *neshamah* also signifies conscious awareness.

The ancient Hebrews were among the first communities to make sustained use of phonetic writing and the first bearers of an alphabet. Unlike other Semitic peoples they did not restrict their use of the alphabet to economic and political record keeping. They used it to record ancestral stories, traditions, and laws, possibly making them the first nation to so thoroughly shift their sensory participation away from the forms of surrounding nature to a purely phonetic set of signs that made them experience profound epistemological independence from the natural environment made possible by this potent new technology. To actively participate with the visible forms of nature came to be considered idolatry by the ancient Hebrews. For them it was not the land, but the written letters that now carried their ancestral wisdom.

Although the Hebrews renounced all animistic engagement with the visible forms of the natural world, whether with the moon, sun, or animals like the bull, which were sacred to other peoples of the Middle East, they retained a participatory relationship with the invisible medium of that world with the wind and the breath.

The power of this relationship can be inferred from the structure of the Hebrew writing system, the *aleph-beth*. This ancient alphabet, in contrast to its European derivatives had no letters for what we call "vowels". The twenty-two letters of the Hebrew *aleph-beth* were all consonants, so to read a text written in traditional Hebrew one had to infer the appropriate vowel sounds from the consonantal context and add them when sounding out the written syllables.

One of the primary reasons for the absence of written vowels in the traditional *aleph-beth* has to do with the nature of vowel sounds themselves. While consonants are shapes made by the lips, teeth, tongue, palate, or throat that momentarily obstruct the flow of breath and gives form to our words and phrases, vowels are those sounds made by unimpeded breath itself.

Vowels are nothing other than sounded breath, and the breath for the ancient Semites was the very mystery of life and awareness inseparable from the invisible *ruach*, holy wind, or spirit. Breath was the vital substance blown into Adam's nostrils by God himself who granted life and consciousness to humankind. It is possible that the Hebrew scribes refrained from creating distinct letters for the vowel sounds in order to avoid making a visible representation of the invisible. To fashion a visible representation of the vowels of the sounded breath would have concretized the ineffable and make a visible likeness of the divine. It would have created a visible representation of a mystery whose essence was to be invisible and unknowable - the sacred breath, the holy wind, so it wasn't done.

The absence of written vowels marks a profound difference between the ancient Semitic *aleph-beth* and the subsequent European alphabets. Unlike texts written with the Greek or the Roman alphabets, a Hebrew text could not be experienced as a substitute for the sensuous, corporal world. The Hebrew letters and texts were not sufficient in and of themselves. In order to be read, they had to be added to, enspirited by the reader's breath. The invisible air, the same mystery that animates the visible terrain was also needed to animate the visible letters to make them come alive and speak. The letters themselves remained dependent upon the elemental corporeal life world that they were activated by, the very breath of that world, and could not be cut off from that world without losing their power.

In this manner the absence of written vowels ensured that Hebrew language and tradition remained open to the power of what exceeded the strictly human community, ensuring that the Hebraic sensibility would remain rooted, however tenuously, in the animate earth. While the Hebrew Bible became a kind of portable Homeland for the Jewish people, it could never take the place of the breathing land itself, upon which the text manifestly depends, hence the persistent themes of exile and longed-for return that reverberate through Jewish history down to the present day.

The absence of written vowels in ancient Hebrew entailed that the reader of a traditional Hebrew text actively choose the appropriate breath sounds or vowels and different vowels frequently varied the meaning of the written consonants.

The apparent precision and efficiency of the new alphabet was obtained at a high price. For by using visible characters to represent the sounded breath, Greek scribes effectively desacralized the breath and the air. By providing a visible representation of that which was by its very nature invisible, they nullified the mysteriousness of the enveloping atmosphere negating the uncanniness of this element that was both here and yet not here, present to the skin, yet absent the eyes, immanence and transcendence all at once.

Plato and Socrates were able to co-opt the term *psyche*, which had been fully associated with the breath and the air, employing it to indicate something not just invisible but intangible. The Platonic *psychê* was not at all a part of the sensuous world, but of another non-sensuous dimension. The *psyche* was no longer an invisible yet tangible power continually participant, by virtue of the breath, with the enveloping atmosphere, but a thoroughly abstract phenomenon now enclosed within the physical body as in a prison.

THE PRISON DOOR CLOSES
ON THE HALL OF MIRRORS

It was only when the unseen air lost its fascination for the human senses that this other, more extreme invisibility took its place, the incorporeal realm of pure "Ideas" that the Platonic rational *psychê* was connected to, much as the earlier breath like *psychê* was joined to the atmosphere.

Wherever the alphabet advanced it dispelled the air of ghosts and invisible influences, essentially stripping the air of its anima, it's psychic depth.

In the oral, animistic world of pre-Christian and peasant Europe, all things, animals, forests, rivers, and caves had the power of expressive speech and the primary medium of this collective discourse was the air. In the absence of writing, human utterance, whether embodied in songs, stories, or spontaneous sounds, it was inseparable from the exhaled breath.

This invisible atmosphere was the de facto intermediary in all communication, a zone of subtle influences crossing, mingling, and metamorphosing. This invisible yet palpable realm of whiffs and scents, vegetative emanations and animal exhalations, was also the unseen repository of ancestral voices, the home of stories yet to be spoken, of ghosts and spirited intelligences; a collective field of meaning from which individual awareness continually emerged and receded with every in and out breath.

This experiential interplay between the seen and the unseen, this duality proper to the sensuous life world was more real for oral people than an abstract dualism between sensuous reality as a whole and some other non-sensuous heaven.

The spread of Christianity was dependent on the spread of the alphabet, and conversely Christian missions and missionaries were the greatest factor in the advancement of alphabetic literacy in both medieval and the modern era. It was not enough to preach the Christian faith, they had to induce unlettered tribal people to use the technology which that faith depended on. Only by training the senses to participate with the written word could anyone hope to break their participation with the animate terrain.

Only as the written text began to speak did the voices of the forest and the river begin to fade, and only then would language loosen its ancient association with the invisible breath, spirit sever itself from the wind, and the psyche dissociate itself from the environment of air. The air, once the medium of expressive interchange became an increasingly empty unnoticed phenomena displaced by the strange new medium of the written word.

The forgetting of the air and the consequent loss of the invisible richness of the present was accompanied by a concurrent internalization of human awareness. We have already examined how the ancient Greek *psyché*, or soul, was transformed from a phenomenon associated with the air in the breath into a holy immaterial entity trapped within the human body. In contact with the written word a new, autonomous, sensibility emerged into experience, a new self that can enter into relation with its own verbal traces and examine its own statements even as it formulates them, allowing it to interact with itself in isolation from other people and from the surrounding animate earth.

This new sensibility independent of the body seems to be from another order entirely, since it is born by the letters and texts whose changeless quality contrasts with the shifting life from the body and the ongoing flux of organic nature. That this new sensibility views itself as an isolated intelligence located "inside" the material body can only be understood in relation to forgetting the air, this sensuous but unseen medium that continually flows in and out of the breathing body, binding the subtle depths within us to the infinite depths that surround us.

The perceptual boundary created by language is porous and permeable and for many oral indigenous people, the boundaries enacted by their language are more like permeable membranes binding them to their particular terrains rather than barriers walling them off from the land. By affirming that other animals have their own languages, and that the rustling of leaves in a maple tree or an aspen grove is itself a kind of voice oral people bind their senses to the shifting sounds and gestures of the local earth and ensure that their own way of speaking remains informed by the life of the land. Still, the membrane enacted by their language is felt and acknowledged as a margin of danger and magic where the relations between the human and more than human worlds must be negotiated. Shamans common to oral cultures dwell precisely on this margin or edge.

The primary role of such magicians is to act as intermediaries between the human and more than human realms by regularly shedding the sensory constraints induced by a common language and dissolving the perceptual boundary to directly encounter, converse, and bargain with various non-human intelligences; with jaguar, condor, or hummingbird, then rejoining the common discourse. In this way shamans keep the human discourse from rigidifying while keeping the perceptual membrane fluid and porous, ensuring the greatest possible attunement between the human community and the animate earth; between the familiar and the infinite.

The advent of *phonetic* writing further rigidified the perceptual boundary enclosing the human community as the written characters were no longer dependent on the larger field of sensuous phenomena, referring instead to a strictly human set of sounds where the letters function as mirrors reflecting the human community back on itself. Nevertheless, even this mirrored boundary can remain open to what lies beyond it.

It was only with the plugging of the last pores with the insertion of visible letters for the vowels themselves that the perceptual boundary established by common language was sealed and the once porous membrane became an impenetrable barrier, creating a hall of mirrors. The Greek scribes transformed the breathing boundary between human culture and the animate earth into a seamless barrier segregating a pure inside from a pure outside. With the addition of written vowels that filled those gaps or pores in the early alphabet, human language became a self-referential system closed off from a larger world that once engendered it, and the "I", the speaking self, was hermetically sealed within this new interior.

Today the speaking self looks out at a purely "exterior" nature from a purely "interior" zone located somewhere inside the physical body or brain. Within alphabetic civilization virtually every human psyche construes itself as just such an individual "interior", a private "mind" or "consciousness" unrelated to the other "minds" surrounding it, or to the environing earth as there is no longer any common medium, no reciprocity, and no *respiration* between the inside and the outside. There is no longer any flow between the self-reflexive domain of alphabetized awareness and all that exceeds, or subtends this determinate realm between consciousness and the unconscious, between civilization and the wilderness.

In the modern world the air has become the most taken for granted of phenomena. Although we continually imbibe it, we fail to notice that there is anything there and refer to the unseen depth between things, people, trees, or clouds as empty space.

Nothing.

The invisibility of the atmosphere, far from leading us to attend to it more closely, enables us to neglect it. Even though we are dependent on its nourishment for all of our thoughts and actions, the immersing medium has no mystery for us and no conscious influence or meaning. Lacking all sacredness and stripped of all spiritual significance, air today is little more than a conveniently forgotten dump site for a host of gaseous effluents and pollutants. Our fascination is elsewhere, carried by newspapers, magazines, radio broadcasts, television networks, and social media, all fields or channels of strictly human communication that readily grab our senses and mold our thoughts once our age-old participation with the original more than human medium has been sundered.

It is the air that most directly envelops us. It is the element that we are most intimately *in*. As long as we experience the invisible depths that surround us as empty space, we can deny our vital interdependence with the other animals, plants, and the living land that sustains us.

The primordial affinity between awareness and the invisible air cannot be avoided. As we become conscious of the unseen depths that surround us, the inwardness or interiority that we associate with the personal psyche begins to be encountered in the world at large and we feel ourselves enveloped, immersed, and caught up *within* the sensual world. This breathing landscape is no longer just a passive backdrop that human history unfolds against, it is a potentized field of intelligence that our actions participate in. As the regime of self-reference breaks down we awaken to the air and to the multiplicitous *Others* that are implicated with us in its generative depths, and the shapes around us appear to come alive.

A story must be judged according to whether it *makes sense*, and "making sense" must be understood in its most direct meaning. To make sense is to *enliven the senses*. A story that makes sense is one that stirs the senses from their slumber and opens the eyes and ears to their real surroundings while tuning the tongue to the actual tastes in the air while sending chills of recognition along the surface of the skin. To *make sense* is to release the body from the constraints imposed by worn out ways of speaking and renew and rejuvenate our felt awareness of the world. It is to make the senses wake up to where they are.

The autonomous mental dimension opened by the alphabet, and the ability to interact with our own signs in total abstraction from our earthly surroundings has blossomed into a vast cognitive realm, a horizonless expanse of virtual interactions and encounters. Our reflective intellects inhabit a global field of information, pondering the latest scenario for the origin of the universe as we absently put food into our mouths, composing presentations for our next meeting while sipping coffee, clicking our mice and slipping into cyberspace to network with other bodiless minds, exchanging information about gene sequences, military coups, or video conferencing to solve global environmental problems, oblivious to the moon rising above our rooftops. With our nervous systems locked in to our keyboards, smart phones, and tablets, and our minds flying about in the infinite hall of mirrors that we have so ingeniously created, we don't notice that the frogs by the nearby stream have dwindled or that fewer song birds have returned to the trees.

In contrast to what appears to us as the unlimited global character of our technologically mediated world, the sensuous world of our direct personal interactions are always local in the particular ground that we walk on and in the air we breathe.

WE LIVE IN A WORLD MADE OF LANGUAGE

Evidence gathered from millennia of shamanic experience argues that the world is made of language whether through the whispering wind, the cries of birds, or the words of our fellow humans spoken from their roots in the ancient form of verbal storytelling, or isolated in the self-contained language of the written word. Although at odds with the expectations of modern science this radical proposition is in agreement with much of current linguistic thinking.

Boston University anthropologist Misia Landau stated that, "The twentieth-century linguistic revolution is the recognition that language is not merely a device for communicating ideas about the world, but rather a tool for bringing the world into existence in the first place. Reality is not simply 'experienced' or 'reflected' in language, but instead is actually produced by language." This is particularly true of traditional oral recitations like the Iliad and the Odyssey, and even more so in the Dreamtime of the aborigines and the oral stories of the Apache.

In *Food of the Gods*, Terence McKenna wrote:

"From the point of view of the psychedelic shaman, the world appears to be more in the nature of an utterance or a tale than in any way related to the leptons and baryons or charge and spin that our high priests, the physicists, speak of. For the shaman, the cosmos is a tale that becomes true as it is told and as it tells itself. This perspective implies that human imagination can seize the tiller of being in the world. Freedom, personal responsibility, and a humbling awareness of the true size and intelligence of the world combine in this point of view to make it a fitting basis for

living an authentic neo-Archaic life. A reverence for and an immersion in the powers of language and communication are the basis of the shamanic path."

The implications of a shamanic point of view take on an even greater meaning in light of our rapidly changing technological world. Einstein's theory of relativity changed the modern concept of reality as we know it. Our perception of the world underwent a radical change from Newtonian physics to relativistic physics, and our collective perception of reality changed as the result of one man's thoughts.

What are thoughts and how are they expressed?

Language.

Uttered and written words are the energy of expressed thoughts. Put them together coherently and storytellers can weave a reality that can be conveyed to others through a common medium that humanity uses as a primary means of communication. This created reality can be an account of a real event made up from the landscape of the mind, imagination, or some combination of the two.

When storytellers create worlds they are the God or Goddess of those worlds in control of the lives and destinies of their creations. If, as shamans believe, there is one unifying universal intelligence manifest in the air that connects us all to each other and the world that we inhabit, then this intelligence is the creator of all that we know. When we choose to create we emulate this force by creating our own universes which we have dominion over, allowing us to *dramatize* our truth, whether "universal" or personal, and put our thoughts in the hearts and minds of others, influencing the way that they perceive reality, possibly changing their reality.

As the Roman alphabet spread through oral Europe, the Old English word spell, which originally meant to simply recite a story, took on a new double meaning. On the one hand, it now meant to arrange in the proper order the written letters that constitute the name of a thing or a person, on the other it signified a magic formula or charm.

To assemble the letters that make up the name of a thing in the correct order was precisely to affect magic and establish a new kind of influence over that entity, to summon it forth! To spell, to correctly arrange the letters to form a name or a phrase, seemed at the same time to cast a spell and exert a new and lasting power over the thing spelled.

To learn to spell was to step under the influence of the written letters ourselves and cast a spell upon our own senses and exchange the wild and multiplicitous magic of an intelligent natural world with the more concentrated and refined magic of the written word.

Make no mistake about it. This is magic. Words *spelled* out with letters create a *spell*. Magicians, shamans, and writers weave spells by working with malleable perception. This is the concept behind what is called "suspension of disbelief", a necessary element of a fiction writer's repertoire, especially in literature of the fantastic.

This magical act of prestidigitation acts as a bridge, bringing forth inner worlds from the minds of their creators through the medium of words, creating a separate reality, or a spell formed by the creator. This classic shamanic journey through infinite inner worlds and the subsequent return "home" forms the basis for Joseph Campbell's Hero's Journey, the cornerstone of what we know as Story which has its roots not only in the original oral tellings of the Illiad and the Odyssey, but also throughout humanity worldwide.

Like the mythical heroes, shamans act as bridges between these worlds. Through strict discipline they learn to free themselves from the restrictions of "ordinary reality", transcending time and space to fly to other worlds and dimensions seeking spiritual knowledge and returning to consensual reality, bringing the wisdom gained from their experience back to this world to share with others. Central to shamanic thought is the concept of transformation which is the essence of the Hero's Journey, the essence of story.

The reason these elements ring true to the core of our being both collectively and individually is because they touch on universal archetypes, in this context defined as statements, patterns of behavior, or prototypes that other statements, patterns of behavior, and objects copy or emulate. They are also Platonic philosophical ideas that refer to pure forms that embody the fundamental characteristics of a thing, a collectively-inherited unconscious idea, pattern of thought, image, etc., that is universally present in individual psyches, or a recurring symbol or motif in literature, painting, or mythology.

Star Wars, ***Harry Potter***, and ***The Lord of the Rings*** as well as other adventures are wildly popular in modern times because the journey of the protagonists in these stories follow the path of the Hero's Journey and hit the archetypes that resonated with their audiences on a deep subconscious level. ***The Iliad***, and ***The Odyssey***

followed this path, as did the creation myths of other cultures, among them "primitive" rain forest tribes. The principles at work in these stories guide the arc of the protagonist and his or her transformation.

The concept of the shaman as a bridge between the worlds is a central idea that defines shamanism. Whether journeying through the spirit world to gain knowledge about healing, or seeking out lost souls in soul retrieval, like the hero on his quest, the shaman must undergo a series of ordeals in the physical, spiritual, and psychological realms to gain access to hidden knowledge that holds the key to power. The Hero's Journey represents a map and a metaphor that shows the way, especially when it comes to rescuing the subpersonalities that we have created and abandoned.

In order to become a man of power, a shaman must travel to the underworld where he faces an ordeal of dismemberment, whether by being swallowed by a jaguar, a common theme in South American shamanism, or some other all-encompassing radical transformation that destroys them like the phoenix in a fire to be reborn in a new more powerful form. This path to destruction and rebirth is referred to as the power path.

In many shamanic cultures, particularly those in the rain forests of South America, the person seeking healing brings their troubles to the shaman. Instead of dispensing medicine to treat the symptoms of the malady the way doctors in the western allopathic model of healing do, *the shaman is often the one who takes the medicine to find a cure for that individual,* allowing them to become the bridge between the spiritual and material worlds.

Understanding the fluid shamanic world view and learning to see things from their perspective brings insight, and no matter what we may believe, the truth is that we create the reality that we experience in our minds where all the inputs we filter are sorted out to bring order to the universe that we are at the center of.

THE HERO'S JOURNEY

Joseph Campbell summarized the steps of the Hero's Journey in his seminal work, *The Hero with a Thousand Faces* and author Christopher Vogler, explored these themes in his popular work, *The Writer's Journey: Mythic Structure For Writers*. Filmmakers like Steven Spielberg, George Lucas, and Francis Coppola owe their successes in part to the ageless pattern of the shaman's journey and path to power that Campbell identified. Popular cultural heroes like Harry Potter, Bilbo and Frodo Baggins, Batman, Superman, Luke Skywalker and many others all follow the Hero's Journey.

All stories can be understood in terms of the hero myth, which has its roots in shamanism and occurs in every culture, in every time, and is as infinitely varied as the human race itself. Stories built on the hero myth have an appeal felt by everyone, because they spring from a universal source in the collective unconscious and reflect universal concerns by dealing with child-like, but universal questions.

Who am I?

Where did I come from?

Where will I go when I die?

What is good and what is evil?

What should I do about it?

What will tomorrow be like?

Where did yesterday go?

Is there anybody else out there?

In *The Writer's Journey: Mythic Structure For Writers* Vogler gave a condensed version of the hero myth and amended it to reflect common themes in movies. What follows is Vogler's amended version with additional comments.

THE STAGES OF THE HERO'S JOURNEY

1.) ORDINARY WORLD

Most stories take us to a special world that is new and alien to its hero. If you're going to tell a story about a fish out of his customary element, you have to create a contrast by showing him in his ordinary world. In STAR WARS we see Luke Skywalker bored to death as a farm boy before he tackles the universe. This is the original place of balance that gets upset and starts the hero on their quest to "reset the balance".

This is the place of normal everyday life where the would be shaman finds themselves prior to "the call".

2.) CALL TO ADVENTURE

Here the hero is presented with a problem, challenge, or adventure. Maybe the land is dying, as in the King Arthur stories about the search for the Grail. In STAR WARS, it's Princess Leia's holographic message to Obi Wan Kenobi, who then asks Luke to join the quest.

In shamanism, it is the first sign from the supernatural that touches them in some way. Shamans can be chosen by odd behaviors or predilections, being struck by lightning and surviving, by interactions with particular plants and animals, great sickness, fever dreams, visions, or some other physiological or psychological crisis.

3.) REFUSAL OF THE CALL

At this point the hero typically balks at the threshold of adventure. He or she is facing the greatest of all fears – fear of the unknown. At this point Luke refuses Obi Wan's call to adventure and returns to his aunt and uncle's farmhouse, only to find they have been barbecued by the Emperor's storm troopers. Suddenly Luke is no longer reluctant, but is eager to undertake the adventure. He is motivated.

At this point the shaman to be struggles with their condition and/or status which makes them uncomfortable and out of place in their old world, yet in fear of the unknown new reality that has come knocking. They walk in a gray area between the worlds, with one foot in the old, and one in the new. Neither of them feels right, forcing them to take steps to "bridge" this gap.

4.) MEETING WITH THE MENTOR

By this time a story will introduce a Merlin-like character who is the hero's mentor. In THE HOBBIT and THE LORD OF THE RINGS it is Gandalf the Wizard. In HARRY POTTER we have another literal wizard in Dumbledore. The mentor gives advice and sometimes magical weapons which is what Obi Wan does when he gives Luke his father's light saber.

The mentor can go so far with the hero, but eventually the hero must face the unknown by themselves. Sometimes the Wise Old Man/Woman is required to give the hero a swift kick in the pants to get the adventure going.

In traditional indigenous societies the only person someone can turn to for help in overcoming a physical, psychological, spiritual crisis is the shaman whose archetype is clearly seen in the wizard, Jedi knight, or sage.

5.) CROSSING THE THRESHOLD

The hero fully enters the special world of the story for the first time. This is the moment where the story takes off and the adventure gets going. The balloon goes up, the romance begins, the spaceship blasts off, the wagon train gets rolling. Dorothy sets out on the Yellow Brick Road. The hero is now committed to his/her journey and there's no turning back.

This is the point where the shaman/acolyte ingests their first visionary plants and/or embarks on their first vision quest which sets them off, isolates them, and singles them out from the rest of their society and puts them in an altered state where the normal rules of life and society no longer apply.

It is the first step into the unknown.

6.) TESTS, ALLIES, ENEMIES

The hero is forced to make allies and enemies in the special world, and has to pass certain tests and challenges that are part of their training. In STAR WARS the cantina is the setting for the forging of an important alliance with Han Solo and the start of an important enmity with Jabba the Hutt. In CASABLANCA Rick's Café is the setting for the "alliances and enmities" phase and in many Westerns it's the saloon where these relationships are tested.

When the shaman's altered state begins, this is where they encounter their shadow which can include allies and guides like power animals, power plants, and elemental spirits, as well as dark, sinister forces from the underworld that challenge them by raising and manifesting their deepest fears.

7.) APPROACH TO THE INMOST CAVE

The hero comes at last to a dangerous place, often deep underground, where the object of the quest is hidden. In the Arthurian stories the Chapel Perilous is the dangerous chamber where the seeker finds the Grail. In many myths the hero has to descend into hell to retrieve a loved one, or into a cave to fight a dragon and gain a treasure. It's Theseus going to the Labyrinth to face the Minotaur. In STAR WARS it's Luke and company being sucked into the Death Star where they will rescue Princess Leia. Sometimes it's just the hero going into his/her own dream world to confront fears and overcome them in an act of personal soul retrieval.

This is the shaman's entry to the crucible where the fires of transformation will destroy the old ego-based paradigms; the jaguar's lair where a huge all-encompassing maw of mortal fear and darkness await. It is the chrysalis where the formless remains of what is no longer relevant awaits its fate.

8.) SUPREME ORDEAL

This is the moment where the hero hits bottom and faces the possibility of death, brought to the brink in a fight with a mythical beast. For the audience standing outside the cave waiting for the victor to emerge it's a black moment. In STAR WARS, it's the harrowing moment in the bowels of the Death Star where Luke, Leia and company are trapped in the giant trash-masher. Luke is pulled under by the tentacled monster that lives in the sewage and is held down so long that the audience begins to wonder if he's dead. IN E.T., THE EXTRATERRESTRIAL, E. T. momentarily appears to die on the operating table.

This is a critical moment in any story, an ordeal where the hero appears to die and be born again and it is a major source of the magic of the hero myth. At this point the audience has been led to identify with the hero and are encouraged to experience the brink-of-death feeling with them. The audience are temporarily depressed, then revived by the hero's return from death.

This is also the magic of any well-designed amusement park thrill ride. Space Mountain or the Great White knuckler make the passengers feel like they're going to die. There's a great thrill that comes with surviving a moment like that.

This is the moment of transformation where the shamanic initiate surrenders the ego and every other aspect of their being to forces greater than him or herself. This is the literal "moment of truth" where they taste death and experience resurrection. You're never more alive than when you think you're going to die.

9.) SEIZING THE SWORD, REWARD

Having survived death, beaten the dragon, slain the Minotaur, the hero now takes possession of the treasure they have come seeking. Sometimes it's a special weapon like a magic sword, a token like the Grail, or some elixir which can heal the wounded land.

The hero may settle a conflict with his father or with his shadowy nemesis. In RETURN OF THE JEDI, Luke is reconciled with both, as he discovers that the dying Darth Vader is his father and not such a bad guy after all.

The hero may also be reconciled with a love interest who is often the treasure they have come to win or rescue, and there is often a love scene or sacred marriage at this point. Women in these stories (or men if the hero is female) tend to be shape-shifters who appear to change in form or age, reflecting the confusing and constantly changing aspects of the opposite sex as seen from the hero's point of view. The hero's supreme ordeal may grant them a better understanding of the opposite sex leading to a reconciliation with them.

At this point, the shaman accepts and embraces their shadow self and begins to integrate both the positive and negative including their fears, insecurities, and numerous other repressed or denied aspects. In Jungian terms this represents individuation.

10.) THE ROAD BACK.

The hero is not out of the woods yet. Some of the best chase scenes come at this point as the hero is pursued by the vengeful forces that he has stolen the elixir or the treasure from. This is the chase as Luke and friends escape from the Death Star with Princess Leia and the plans that will bring down Darth Vader.

If the hero has not yet managed to reconcile with his father or the gods, they may come raging after him at this point. This is the moonlight bicycle flight of Elliott and E. T. as they escape from "Keys" (Peter Coyote), a force representing governmental authority. By the end of the movie Keys and Elliott have been reconciled and it even looks like Keys will end up as Elliott's step-father.

In the shaman's world this is where the scattered subpersonalities of the ego, spirit, and essence are reintegrated in a new way with a world view that is completely different from the old one. This new "enlightened" perspective is enhanced as a result of the fear embracing act of transformation and imbued with the personal power and knowledge that the shaman has earned by accepting and acknowledging his shadow.

11.) RESURRECTION

The hero emerges from the special world transformed by their experience. There is often a replay here of the mock death-and-rebirth of Stage 8 as the hero once again faces death and survives. The Star Wars movies play with this theme constantly – all three of the original films feature a final battle scene in which Luke is almost killed, appears to be dead for a moment, then miraculously survives, transformed into a new being by his experience.

Here the shaman returns as a man or woman of power. As part of the initiation this transformed being is challenged anew by the negative antagonistic forces that started their quest to reset the balance. In this confrontation they overcome their opposition, empowered by their new found power and knowledge, proving to themselves and subsequently to the world that they have won out over the forces of darkness.

12.) RETURN WITH THE ELIXIR

The hero comes back to the ordinary world, but the adventure would be meaningless unless they brought back the elixir, treasure, or some lesson from the special world. Sometimes it's just knowledge or experience, but they have to come back with the elixir or some boon to mankind, or they're doomed to repeat the adventure until they do. Many comedies use this ending, as a foolish character refuses to learn his lesson and embarks on the same folly that got him in trouble in the first place.

Sometimes the boon is treasure won on the quest, love, or just the knowledge that the special world exists and can be survived. Sometimes it's simply coming home with a good story to tell.

This is the reason that shamans are referred to as bridges. Their task is to travel the realms of spirit and visit other dimensions and realities that are incomprehensible to the uninitiated and return with the knowledge and wisdom gained there to benefit and heal those in need.

Plato's "Parable of the Cave" provides a great metaphor for the gap in perception that a shaman/hero must bridge to share the "elixir". In this tale Plato has Socrates describe a gathering of people who have lived chained to the wall of a cave all of their lives facing a blank wall.

The people watch shadows projected on the wall by things passing in front of a fire behind them, and begin to designate names to these shadows, which are as close as the prisoners get to viewing reality. He then explains how the philosopher (shaman/hero) is like a prisoner who is freed from the cave and comes to understand that the shadows on the wall do not make up reality at all, as he can perceive the true form of reality rather than the mere shadows seen by the prisoners.

The hero's attempts to articulate this new found expanded view of reality is incomprehensible to those still chained to the wall as they have no precedent to gauge it by, so the hero must strive to "bridge the worlds" in whatever way they can to share the wisdom that they have risked everything to learn on their adventure outside the bounds of what is known.

In summary: The hero is introduced in their ORDINARY WORLD where they receive the CALL TO ADVENTURE. They are RELUCTANT at first to CROSS THE FIRST THRESHOLD where they encounter TESTS, ALLIES and ENEMIES. They reach the INNERMOST CAVE where they endure the SUPREME ORDEAL, then they SEIZE THE SWORD or treasure and is pursued on the ROAD BACK to their world. They are RESURRECTED and transformed by their experience and RETURN to their ordinary world with a treasure, boon, or ELIXIR to benefit their world.

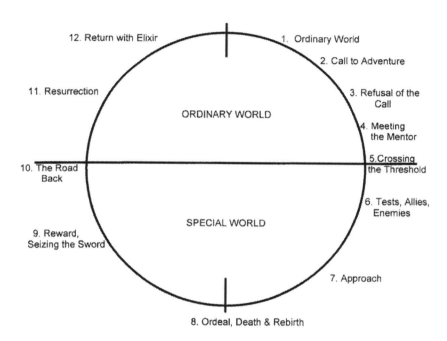

THE HERO'S JOURNEY

From Vogler's *"The Writer's Journey: Mythic Structure For Writers"*

THE MOVING CRUCIBLE

From an energetic standpoint, up and down, back and forth, dark and light; the dance of two polarities, each dependent on the other, shift frequency and amplitude according to the fluctuating rhythms of the unfolding story of our lives. There can be no light without darkness to set it off against and up cannot exist without down.

The hero's journey that we live and act out in our day to day lives centers around our relationships, good, bad, and everything in between. We never know our own or another person's true mettle until they are in conflict.

There are many truths about storytelling, whether oral or written that provide the archetype that has its origins in shamanic transformation. One of the central facts of this journey is that *character is revealed through conflict*. Under pressure personalities will unfold, showing themselves, their fears, passions and intentions. The greater the conflict the greater the polarity in forces which translates into more energy, meaning a greater potential for more radical change. This high concentration of energy is the crucible of transformation that holds the greatest potential.

Examining the roots of the words that characterize these forces helps to define the energies at work within this crucible. In storytelling terms the basis of the words protagonist and antagonist come from **agonist,** a chemical that binds to a receptor, activating it to produce a biological response. In essence, an agonist causes an action, and an antagonist blocks the action of the agonist. To put it in simpler terms an agonist is something that initiates a response.

126

In literary, metaphorical, psychological, and shamanic terms, the antagonist represents the shadow.

In this activity, the word thesis and antithesis come from the noun **synthesis** which refers to a combination of two or more entities that when combined together form something new. The corresponding verb, **synthesize** means *to make or form a synthesis*, which is the essence of transformation.

The Transformative Moment

When a shaman descends into the underworld to undergo transformation by dismemberment, or to be, "swallowed by the jaguar", they are in effect being swallowed by their shadow, which is the equivalent of psychological dismemberment, or the "ordeal, death, and rebirth" in The Hero's Journey. In shamanic lore it is a bid for power and power is the reward for surviving this terrifying encounter, characterized in The Hero's Journey by the "seizing of the sword".

In shamanism and in the more revealing and sometimes fantastical parts of the hero's journey as well as in life, the shadow can appear in dreams, visions, and in other forms, including human. Its appearance and role depend on the living experience of the individual because much of the shadow was created and developed in the individual's mind rather than being inherited in the collective unconscious. Some Jungian psychologists maintain that '*The shadow* contains, besides the personal shadow, the shadow of society, fed by the neglected and repressed collective values'.

Jung also made the suggestion of more than one layer making up the shadow. The top layers contain the meaningful flow and manifestations of direct personal experiences made unconscious in the individual by such things as the change of attention from one thing to another, forgetfulness, or repression. Underneath these idiosyncratic layers are the archetypes that form the psychic contents of all human experiences. Jung described this deeper layer as "a psychic activity which goes on independently of the conscious mind and is not dependent even on the upper layers of the unconscious—untouched, and perhaps untouchable by personal experience." This bottom layer of the shadow is what Jung referred to as the collective unconscious.

This encounter with the shadow is what happens in the soul retrieval of these subpersonalities which plays a central part in the process of synthesis and transformation within the crucible. Jung stated that this course of individuation exhibits a formal regularity. Its signposts and milestones are archetypal symbols marking its stages, and of these the first stage leads to the experience of the SHADOW.

In Jung's words, "The shadow personifies everything that the subject refuses to acknowledge about himself" and represents "a tight passage, a narrow door, whose painful constriction no one is spared who goes down to the deep well". This tight passage is in fact the birth canal that must be passed through, "the road back" in the Hero's Journey that leads to "Resurrection", which is rebirth coming from the death of the ego.

The dissolution of the persona and the launch of the individuation process also bring with it the danger of falling victim to the black shadow that everybody carries with them as the inferior and hidden aspect of the personality. In Obi-Wan-Kenobi's vernacular, it is the dark side of the force.

The shadow sometimes overwhelms a person's actions like when the conscious mind is shocked, confused, or paralyzed by indecision. Jung said that, "A man who is possessed by his shadow is always standing in his own light and falling into his own traps ... living below his own level. In terms of the story of Dr. Jekyll and Mr. Hyde." It must be Jekyll, the conscious personality who integrates the shadow and *not* vice versa. Otherwise the conscious becomes the slave of the autonomous shadow.

On the road home the hero or shaman travels back through healing *spirals*. Here the struggle is to retain *awareness* of the shadow, but not identification with it. Non-identification demands considerable moral effort and prevents a descent into that darkness. Though the conscious mind is liable to be submerged at any moment in the unconscious, understanding or witness consciousness acts like a life-saver by integrating the unconscious and reincorporating the shadow into the personality, producing a stronger, wider consciousness than before, individuation in Jungian terms and the definition of personal power in shamanism.

All of this is to say that the dynamic moving crucible at the center of a story, wherever the story moment in the unfolding narrative of life is at the moment of scrutiny, manifests a self-aware transforming, evolving energy that not only fills the shaman-hero, but *is* the shaman hero in the same way that the Apache and the aborigines maintain their intimate relationship between land and human, inseparable from songs and stories.

This active communication is also inseparable from the shapes and features of the land, and the chanting of song cycles links the human singer to the animals, plants, or powers within the landscape.

As discussed, "externally", the invisible Air is the intermediary in all communication, providing a zone of subtle influences that cross, mingle, and metamorphose. This invisible realm holds a collective field of meaning that individual awareness emerges from and recedes into with every in and out breath.

Within this medium, sound waves are generated by vibrating structures from plants and animals, and in our own bodies by our vocal cords, our primary instruments of communication.

On an olfactory level, plants communicate with us from a distance by their varied aromas and on a visual level attract us by their stunning beauty or they repel us by scents, thorns, or other sensory antagonists.

When shamans ingest particular plants, they subject themselves to the energy field of those plants which affect them in mysterious ways on multiple levels that can scarcely be comprehended. Through the subjective experiences that they produce in us plants communicate in ways that defy logic and articulation.

When we experience language, regardless of its form as more than a device for communicating ideas about the world, but a tool for bringing it into existence, reality is not just 'experienced' or 'reflected' in language, it is *produced* by language."

For the shaman, the cosmos is a tale that becomes true as it is told and as it tells itself, which implies that human imagination in the form of "witness consciousness" can seize the tiller of being in the world, bringing freedom, personal responsibility, and a humbling awareness of the true size and intelligence of the cosmos along with a reverence for and immersion in the powers of language and communication, which are the basis of the shamanic path.

In visionary states information is communicated internally in a nonrational way through alien feeling symbols, concepts, emotions, thoughts, vistas, and other mixed, often synesthetic perceptions that contain dense information that often unfolds through transforming geometric colors and patterns.

Not only do these mesmerizing multi-hued geometric mathematical permutations constitute a unique language primarily available to the inner perception of the human mind, but geometry in and of itself is a universal language containing self-apparent truths, regardless of any differences in the spoken language of the perceiver.

Historically, Galileo asserted that only those properties of matter that are directly amenable to mathematical measurement, such as size, shape, and weight are real while the other more subjective qualities like sound, taste, and color are merely illusionary impressions, since the book of nature is written in the language of mathematics alone. In his words:

"The grand book the universe... is written in the language of mathematics and its characters are triangles, circles, and other geometric figures without which it is humanly impossible to understand a single word of it; without these, one wanders about in a dark Labyrinth."

Though Galileo may have missed the mark regarding the measurement of the "subjective qualities" of sound, taste, and color in light of modern day methods that measure what he could not perceive with the technology of his day, there is great truth in his comments about the language of mathematics and geometry which shamans have always known as the universal language that it is.

GETTING TO THE POINT

Nothing is a concept denoting the absence of something, and is associated with *nothingness,* the state of being nothing, the state of nonexistence of anything, or the property of having nothing. This is how "non-believing" atheists characterize any conception of God, yet in the paradox of their denial they are unequivocally announcing that *they themselves are God* as they have made the ultimate judgment call, and in so doing they claim their throne at the center of their universe located right between their eyes.

From this perspective, if they suddenly ceased to exist then nothing else would exist either, (for them), which not only makes them a creator God who rules over the existence of everything that falls under their range of thought and perception, it denies existence to any other unique and individual intelligences that exist "outside" of them.

The idea that God created the universe out of nothing (*creatio ex nihilo*) became central to Judaism, Christianity, and Islam. With the exception of the metaphorical wind moving over the water that hinted at this in the first sentence of the Hebrew Bible, this concept is not found directly in Genesis, nor in the entire Hebrew Bible. The authors of Genesis 1, writing around 500–400 BCE, were not concerned with the origins of matter (the material which God formed into the habitable cosmos), but with the fixing of destinies. This was still the situation in the early 2nd century CE, although early Christian scholars were beginning to see a tension between the idea of world-formation and the omnipotence of God. By the beginning of the 3rd century this tension was resolved, world-formation was overcome, and creation *ex nihilo* became a fundamental tenet of Christian theology.

Ex nihilo is a Latin phrase meaning "out of nothing" and often appears in conjunction with the concept of creation, as in *creatio ex nihilo*, meaning "creation out of nothing", chiefly in philosophical or theological contexts, but it also occurs in other fields.

In theology, the common phrase *creatio ex nihilo* contrasts with *creatio ex materia* (creation out of some pre-existent, eternal matter) and with *creatio ex deo* (creation out of the being of God). *Creatio continua* is the ongoing divine creation.

The phrase *ex nihilo* also appears in the classical philosophical formulation *ex nihilo nihil fit*, which means "Out of nothing comes nothing".

When used outside of religious or metaphysical contexts *ex nihilo* also refers to something coming from nothing. For example, in a conversation, one might raise a topic *"ex nihilo"* if it bears no relation to the previous topic of discussion.

As explored earlier, one of the most sacred magical respected elemental spirits among tribal cultures is the Wind, an invisible force capable of unfathomable power that has no substance, yet is defined as not only a direct link to spirit, but *spirit itself* manifest as formless, invisible, energy. We have no perception of it when it is at rest and we perceive and characterize it as *nothing* as it registers nothing with any of our senses, making it a perceptual enigma, yet it is the most pervasive presence we know.

We cannot speak, act, or think without its participation and this unseen enigma holds the mystery that enables life to live and unites our breathing bodies to the world around us and to the interior life of all that we perceive in the open field of this living presence.

In shamanic thought the air is the soul of the visible landscape that constitutes the secret realm where all beings draw their nourishment from, and yet it is that most intimate absence felt and characterized as *nothing*.

Nothing is more common to the diverse indigenous cultures of the earth than a recognition of the air, the wind, and the breath as aspects of a singularly sacred power. By virtue of its pervading presence, its invisibility and its influence on all manner of visible phenomena, the air is the archetype of all that is ineffable, unknowable, yet undeniably real and efficacious. Many indigenous people construe awareness not as a power that resides inside their heads, but as a quality that they themselves are inside of.

All of this can be defined as a void, meaning a completely empty space. The contradictory fact that void is defined as a noun, which by definition is a person, place, or thing, means that we have defined nothing as something, which is nothing. This puzzling contradictory definition also encompasses the term point, (which has no dimension), zero, and spirit (formless and invisible), which all mean the same thing.

Zero-point or **ground state energy** is considered the lowest possible energy that a quantum mechanical system can have. Unlike classical mechanics quantum systems constantly fluctuate in their lowest energy state due to the Heisenberg uncertainty principle. According to modern physics the universe can be thought of not as isolated particles but continuous fluctuating fields: matter fields, whose quanta are fermions (i.e. leptons and quarks), and force fields, whose quanta are bosons (e.g. photons and gluons). All these fields have zero-point energy and these fluctuating zero-point fields lead to a reintroduction of an aether in physics.

Physics currently lacks a full theoretical model for understanding zero-point energy, in particular the discrepancy between theorized and observed vacuum energy which has become a source of major contention. Physicists Richard Feynman and John Wheeler calculated the zero-point radiation of the vacuum to be an order of magnitude greater than nuclear energy, with one teacup containing enough energy to boil all the world's oceans, yet according to Einstein's theory of general relativity any such energy would gravitate, and the experimental evidence from both the expansion of the universe, dark energy, and the Casimir effect (A small attractive force that acts between two close parallel uncharged conducting plates due to quantum vacuum fluctuations of the electromagnetic field.), show any such energy to be exceptionally weak.

If supersymmetry is valid at all, it is at most a broken symmetry, only true at very high energies, and no one has been able to show a theory where zero-point cancellations occur in the low energy universe we observe today. This discrepancy is known as the cosmological constant problem, one of the greatest unsolved mysteries in physics.

In mathematics, **"0"** is the integer immediately preceding 1 and it is an even number because it is divisible by 2 with no remainder. 0 is neither positive nor negative. By most definitions it is the only natural number not to be positive. Zero is a number which quantifies a count or an amount of null size. In most cultures, 0 was identified before the idea of negative things where quantities less than zero were accepted.

The number 0 is the smallest non-negative integer. The natural number following 0 is 1 and no natural number precedes 0. The number 0 may or may not be considered a natural number, but it is a whole number and hence a rational number and a real number as well as an algebraic number and a complex number.

The number 0 is neither positive nor negative and is usually displayed as the central number in a number line. It is neither a prime number nor a composite number. It cannot be prime because it has an infinite number of factors, and cannot be composite because it cannot be expressed as a product of prime numbers. Zero must always be one of the factors, but it is however, even as well as being a multiple of any other integer, rational, or a real number. A common paradox occurs with mathematical idealizations such as point sources which describe physical phenomena well at distant or global scales but break down at the point itself.

These paradoxes are sometimes seen as relating to Zeno's paradoxes which all deal with the physical manifestations of mathematical properties of continuity, infinitesimals, as well as and infinities associated with space and time. For example, the electric field associated with a point charge is infinite at the location of the point charge. A consequence of this paradox is that the electric field of a point-charge can only be described in a limiting sense by a carefully constructed Dirac delta function. This mathematically inelegant but physically useful concept allows for the efficient calculation of the associated physical conditions while conveniently sidestepping the philosophical issue of what actually occurs at the infinitesimally-defined point: a question that physics is as yet unable to answer.

In Euclidean geometry, a point is a primitive notion that the geometry is built upon. Being a primitive notion means that a point cannot be defined in terms of previously defined objects. That is, a point is defined only by some properties called axioms that it must satisfy. In particular geometric points do not have any length, area, volume, or any other dimensional attribute. A common interpretation is that the concept of a point is meant to capture the notion of a unique location in Euclidean space.

Points, considered within the framework of Euclidean geometry are one of the most fundamental objects. Euclid originally defined the point as "that which has no part".

There are several inequivalent definitions of dimension in mathematics and in all of the common definitions, a point is zero dimensional.

Like the Wind, the Air, and the Nothing that gives us existence, there are no physical proofs of electricity, magnetism, or gravity, yet the tangible proof of their existence is inherent in the invisible world around us that provides the medium that they travel through. They exist as manifestations and forms of energy, and though we cannot see their forms we can see and harness their effects.

It is interesting to note in terms of energy that we cannot see emotions, especially in others, but we can perceive their effects inside ourselves, and the emotional perception and empathy we experience from being tuned in to emotions and being heart centered indicates where essence meets the world, and that is the point.

FROM HERE TO INFINITY

The divine is evident in the first sentence of the Hebrew Bible describing the beginning of Hebrew creation when (time) and where (space) God is present as the wind moving over the waters, and in the breath of life blown into Adam's nostrils, awakening him. Just as in this creation myth, in the three dimensional reality that we inhabit, everything that evolves must have a beginning where all that manifests comes into being. This nexus is defined as the point of origin where the intangible becomes tangible and the first duality that defines our existence comes into play. This infinity point is the basis for our dualistic three dimensional world view that plays out endlessly in the way that we perceive it.

Spirit-matter, subject-object, positive-negative, yin-yang, male-female, day-night, sleeping-waking, and life-death are a small sampling of the dual archetype that provides the basis for life. It manifests in the inhale-exhale of our lungs, the beating of our hearts, the ticking of our clocks, our music in the primal beats of a drum, and the notes which would not be differentiated without the spaces between them. Two is also the basis for our world wide computerization and it's web of information, based on the simple binary notation of ones and zeroes. The permutations of duality are endless, but to understand its origins we need to get to the point, where it all begins.

.

A point has no size and can only be imagined. It fixes a location in space and has a dimension equal to zero. If you take a point and move it from its original location to another location, this moving point creates a line which constitutes the first dimension known as length.

This movement is a manifestation of energy, which is the essence of consciousness -- the proverbial wind on the water.

When we move a line which has no thickness from its original location to another location, it leaves the first dimension and becomes a plane which has two dimensions, length and width.

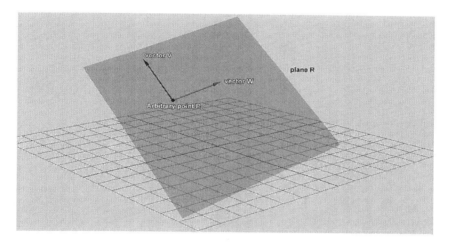

When we move a plane, it leaves two dimensions and creates a solid body with three dimensions, length, width, and height. If each of these dimensional shifts cover the same distance, the result is a cube, the basic representation of three dimensional reality represented by 2^2, known as two to the second power, or two cubed.

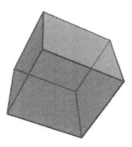

When you move a three dimensional body in space, it remains a three dimensional body and does not leave the third dimension.

If you imagine yourself without any dimensions you would be formless. Zero dimension is the point, the first dimension indicating energetic movement is the line, the second dimension is the surface, and the third dimension is the solid body. If you imagine yourself as a being who can only move along the first dimension of a straight line, all you would see is points, not your own dimensionality, because when we attempt to draw something within a one dimensional line, points are the only option.

A two-dimensional being moving through a plane would encounter lines and thus distinguish one-dimensional beings and a three-dimensional being within a cube would encounter planes and perceive two dimensional beings. Human beings however, can perceive three-dimensions.

A one-dimensional being can perceive only points, a two-dimensional being only one dimension, and a three-dimensional being only two dimensions. By the logic of this progression it becomes apparent that the perception of each dimension necessitates being one dimension above it, therefore human beings who can delineate external beings in three dimensions and manipulate three-dimensional spaces must be four dimensional beings. Just as being within a cube can perceive only two dimensions and not its own third dimension, it is also true that human beings cannot perceive the fourth dimension in which we live.

The movement of the point to make the line, the line to the plane, and the plane to the solid all take time, making time synonymous with movement. We perceive the energetic movement of our three dimensional bodies through space as time. How long does it take to get from point A to point B? Our whole concept of time and our calendar is based on physical movement, specifically by counting the number of identical cyclical movements that a particular time measurement corresponds to.

It takes three hundred and sixty five and a quarter days for the earth to circle the sun in a solar year, one month for the moon to circle the earth, a day of twenty four hours for the earth to complete a rotation on its axis, sixty minutes to make up an hour, and sixty seconds to make up a minute. Our materialistic world view has us locked in to time perception based on the movement of physical bodies through space, but what of the source of the expansion and its point of origin that make up the other unseen formless half of the formula?

This formless half of the formula comes from inside of us where the seat of consciousness resides, perched between subject and object in an infinity zone where the evolution of consciousness takes place. A shift in our perceptions brings a shift in how we live in and perceive the world from our present fourth dimensional existence that perceives a three dimensional world, to fifth dimensional existence where we perceive the fourth dimension, transcending time and duality.

New discoveries in quantum physics lay the ground for this by proving that matter is more empty space than solidity. In terms of Einstein's famous $E=MC^2$, matter is another form of energy, and energy is the essence of consciousness. The fundamental nature of this paradox tells us that positive and negative are extremes. It is the energy between them that matters. That is where the action is and where we exist within ourselves; at the threshold of subject and object, in the center, mid-point of our duality. When we transcend the poles, we become centered and rise above the opposition of forces to embrace the energy that they manifest.

When the mid-point rises above the baseline, its transcendence creates a triad, trinity, or triangle. The three dimensional representation of a triangle with four sides creates a pyramid, one of the greatest enigmas known to mankind. The square base of a pyramid represents the four dimensions and the four directions of the physical world and rises up pointing toward the heavens in a diminishing apex that represents an infinity point where matter ends and spirit begins.

Similar to the example of the pyramid, the laws of geometry are self evident when moving from three dimensional space to fourth dimensional time through the study of projective geometry.

Euclidean geometry describes shapes as they are. Their properties of length, angles, and parallelism are unchanged by rigid motions.

Projective geometry describes objects as they appear. Lengths, angles, and parallelism become distorted when we look at objects from this perspective which provides a mathematical model for how images of the 3 dimensional world are formed.

Projective geometry is the branch of mathematics that deals with the relationships between geometric figures and the images, or mappings that come from projecting them onto another surface. Common examples are the shadows cast by opaque objects and motion pictures displayed on a screen.

As shown below, the eye is connected to points on the landscape of the horizontal reality plane, *RP*, by sight lines. The intersection of these lines with the vertical picture plane, *PP* generates the drawing, projecting the reality plane onto the picture plane, hence the name *projective* geometry.

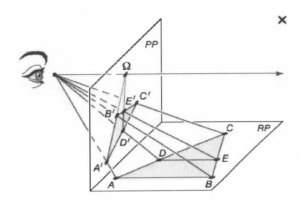

Counter space is the space where subtle forces not amenable to ordinary measurement work. Instead of having its ideal elements in a plane at infinity it has them in a "point at infinity". They are lines and planes rather than lines and points as in ordinary space, and are known as *counter space infinity*. A plane incident with it is said to be an *ideal plane* or *plane at infinity* in counter space. It only appears for a different peripheral kind of consciousness that experiences such a point as infinite inwardness that is in contrast to normal consciousness that experiences infinite outwardness.

In counter space terms this infinity point is known as a linkage; an element that belongs to both Euclidian and counter space at once, such as a point or plane. If a cube is linked to both spaces at once, and is moved upward away from the inner infinitude, it will obey the metrics of both spaces. The diagram below shows what happens as it moves. The smaller version obeys space and stays the same size and shape in space, while the bigger version obeys the counter space metric.

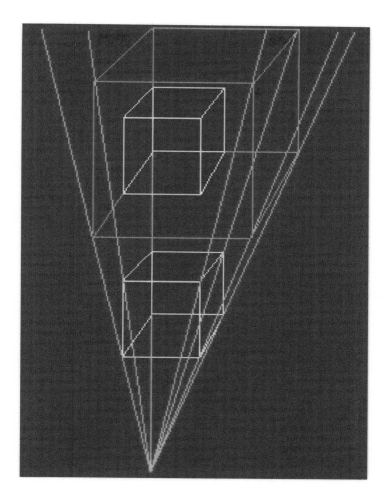

The counter space or inner infinity is shown as a point at the bottom. Lines drawn from it through the vertices of the cube stay on these lines, obeying its metric properties, illustrated by the smaller cube while the smaller spatial cube stays the same spatially. This seems natural with our ordinary consciousness, but for counter space consciousness the other is most natural and the projected cube appears to be getting bigger.

The geometric difference between the two cubes is referred to as *strain,* analogous to the use of that term in engineering where it is the percentage deformation in size, like when a rubber band is stretched. The rubber band responds to the strain by exerting a force referred to as *stress.*

The central principles here are:

1.)   Objects may be linked to both spaces at once.
2.)   When they are, strain arises when they move because the metrics are coflicting.
3.)   Stress arises as a result of the strain.

Stress is not a geometric concept. We move from geometry to physics when we consider it. The major stress free movement or transformation is rotation about an axis through the counter space infinity. This focal "power point" axis that is the core of stress free movement and transformation is the infinity zone, the point where we transcend polarities and become centered.

HOW THE COSMIC MOTHER
AND FATHER GIVE BIRTH

Gurdjieff stated that pure knowledge cannot be transmitted, but by being expressed in symbols it is covered by them as by a veil, but for those who desire and who know how to look this veil becomes transparent. Regardless of the multiple forms of verbal expression throughout the world, geometry is solid, observable self-apparent truth in a universal language that articulates itself in dynamic unfolding progressions that map the pathways of manifesting reality.

Dimensionality is always dictated by geometric expansion and contraction, whether opening itself out into the infinite macrocosm or moving down through the equally infinite holographic microcosm.

This first movement from zero point to a line is that same first movement of the cosmic breath upon the waters of creation and in this first movement not only is One created from zero, but the energy that created that state is evident within the two new polarities that contain it. When these polarities are transcended the paradox of their opposites is overcome, opening the progression up to more expanded levels of expression, and when they work together at this basic level of duality, we have one and zero which among other things in the natural world is the basis for human logic that dictates not only the form and function of our world wide web of computers, but our entire monetary and business network.

What used to be backed by gold, one of the densest elements, is now many times removed and diluted from its original representation as promissory notes, to a series of ones and zeros, nothing more than a changing state of energy, one or zero, on or off, yes or no.

143

This duality permeates our existence with the beating of our hearts, the in and out of our breaths, the two sides of our bilateral brains, the rising and setting of the sun and moon, and in the interplay of masculine and feminine energies that make life as we know it possible. Shamans honor this most primal pulse of life and being through the beats of their drum, which is considered and extension of their heart.

This initial singular movement of a point into a line begins the one-dimensional angular progression of dimensionality from the zero point of manifestation out through the three dimensions of length, width, and height, which define our consensual perception of reality. These straight line angled expressions that we see in the two dimensions of squares and rectangles and the three dimensions of cubes and boxes represent the Cosmic Masculine.

If we go back once more to the zero point of origin, and extend it out equally from its central location in every direction on the same plane that we extended the line on, we create a two dimensional circle, and if we extend the point out equally in every possible direction we have a three dimensional sphere that represents the Cosmic Feminine.

Ancient cultural examples of this prehistoric truth are evident on the island of Amantani situated on Lake Titicaca in Peru, close to the Bolivian border. Amantani is said to be a mystical power place because of the ancient temples located there. The island is about 9.28 kilometers in size and home to about 3700 people, and basically consists of 2 mountains with an ancient temple on each peak; the mother earth temple of Pachamama, dedicated to the feminine aspect of the universe and the father earth temple of Pachatata, dedicated to the masculine aspect.

The inhabitants of the island who belong to the ancient Aymara culture say that the temples are more than 4000 years old. To reach them one follows a path from the lake up to the temples through stone arches reputed to act as initiatory gateways. At some point there is a plateau with a crossroad that has one path going to the temple of Pachatata and the other one to the temple of Pachamama.

The masculine temple of Pachatata is very distinct sitting right on its peak in a square form while the temple of Pachamama has a round shape and the mountain where it is located is more diverse as it is more open and wide.

Both temples have a very different energy. At Pachatata many people experience a sense of clarity, centeredness, inner strength and report a connection with their higher selves. At Pachamama they experience a deeper sense of beauty, love, nourishment, and connection with the earth. These are also characteristics often described as masculine and feminine.

Other deeply embedded masculine and feminine qualities follow these circular and angular geometric indicators of gender in both the human and animal kingdoms, further reinforcing this observation. When a man concentrates on a particular task he remains quiet with a single minded focus to the exclusion of all else, reinforcing the point to line directness, while women multitask, and "gossip" with each other, employing necessary skills for their survival.

These habits are deeply embedded in human and animal behaviors, particularly mammals. A male hunter must be quiet, direct, and often solitary to be successful, while women, out of biological necessity must not only keep the nest, they must be aware of everything that goes on around them and around any other nest keepers in the vicinity to survive. Aside from keeping a watchful eye over their offspring, their multitasking and communicative chatter is an essential skill for the gathering part of the hunter gatherer paradigm.

All anyone needs to do to confirm this is to observe the differences in the way a man or woman shops. A man goes straight for his beer and his steak, then he is out of there, while a woman typically goes from item to item, gathering, often drawn from one thing to the next by distraction.

On another note, the two basic fears that humans have are divided between the sexes. Women, who are vulnerable because of the position and dependence that child bearing puts upon them fear abandonment, while men who must be solitary and independent fear entrapment.

The sacred feminine circle carries high value in tribal societies. Structures are built round, tribal councils are held in circles, and medicine wheels are circular, all honoring the sun, moon, and the life giving circles evident in the seasons, orbits, and endlessly repeating cycles of nature.

The Emerald Tablet written by Hermes Trismegistus contained the secret of transmutation of primordial substance. The tablet text contains the famous lines "As above, so below" and goes on to explain creation in the context of duality. Understanding the duality of the masculine and the feminine is the key. Much of this wisdom has been lost through the ages resulting in grand misconceptions of what actually constitutes the masculine and feminine in their archetypal forms. Understanding these forces is more important now than ever, for it is the misunderstanding and the resultant extreme polarization of these forces that threatens life on earth as we know it. It is mastery of both of these forces and the synthesis of the two that creates growth, advancement, and value fulfillment.

Fundamentally, the masculine and the feminine are NOT two tangible separate things. They both exist on the same continuum and are very real forces having different directions while being inexplicably linked. One cannot exist without the other in any meaningful way, and for that matter no polarity whether considered masculine, feminine, positive, negative, light or dark can exist without its opposite.

Categorically the feminine and masculine can best be understood as forces or tendencies in the following ways:

Masculine — Feminine

Projective — Receptive
Expansive — Contractive
Heating — Cooling
Sympathetic — Parasympathetic
Intellectual — Emotional
Outward — Inward
Brighter — Darker
Yang — Yin
Magnetic — Dielectric
Square — Circle

The sun is a burning hot fire that radiates it's energy in all directions, making it the archetypal masculine in almost every way making "Father Sun" an apt description. The earth on the other hand is archetypal feminine, referred to as "Mother Earth", mostly a dark blue water & black soil planet that receives the bright masculine rays from the sun, making the sun projective and the earth receptive. The sun is above and the earth is below and life/creation occurs in-between.

In the Taoist system yang is white symbolizing the projective light of the sun and yin is black symbolizing the receptive earth.

Yin and Yang Symbol

It is interesting to note that the color green is in the middle of the visible spectrum. Green is the color of life on earth and represents the meeting point between the red fire of the masculine and the cool nurturing blue of the feminine. Plants nourish themselves from water and soil in the ground (feminine) and send their branches and leaves out skyward for nourishment from the sun (masculine). Trees and how they function are highly symbolic of these primordial forces, being the creative point in the delicate balance state between these two.

The process of clouds condensing to cooler water and coming down from the sky and nourishing/replenishing life on earth is the *feminine act of cooling, soothing and rejuvenating.*

In the human body arteries carry blood which is red (masculine) when oxygenated and the veins are purple/blue (feminine) and are depleted of the oxygen yet receptive to it in the lungs for replenishment.

The Taoist system explains the story of creation from primordial source Wu-Chi which literally means "without ridgepole" and is considered an infinite boundless state of no differentiation. The dot in the middle is the point of yin from which creation begins to emerge. The forces of yin then contract the yang to form a state of rotating force-balance or Tai Chi which literally means "great pole". Yang is a universal expansionary force of continuous rapid replication and yin is a contractive force that contracts rotationally in order to create reality.

Creation is an **emergent** property of the interplay between masculine and feminine. The story of creation is fundamentally a story of movement from non-duality/polarity to duality/polarity.

The Biblical parallel to the Taoist system of the creation of masculine and feminine is the story of how feminine Eve was created from a rib from the side of masculine Adam, and also how light, (yang) was the first creation, then all forms of matter (yin) and life were created after.

The cosmological analogy is that in the early part of the theoretical "big bang" the universe existed in a super hot state of expanding plasma, a masculine process, and then through a feminine process in the formation of matter, planets, and stars that came through a process of coalescing and cooling.

Hyper-dimensionally the expansionary and contractory nature of the universe goes out to infinity both inward and outward and there is no beginning or end, thus no first or last.

The birth of polarity in its archetypal form is the most fundamental necessity for existence of any kind, for without it no frameworks could be created. The feminine represents detailed refinement and a move toward ever increasingly complexity and novelty in a higher order manner.

A CHILD IS BORN

As stated earlier the square providing structure is the archetypal male and the curve or circle is the archetypal female. In nature this is exemplified through hurricanes or tornadoes and the ensuing vortex is inherently the geometry of how matter is created through a geometric contraction process of what is called curving the square where the squares unfold outward to infinity while the curve rotates inward to infinity. Squares provide the matrix like substrate -- the primordial universal tapestry, and the the act of curving and twisting the squares is the feminine process of creation. This is why the Fibonacci ratio and golden spiral is inherent in all natural systems. This whole inner and outer bidirectional process is guided by what is variously called the golden mean, the divine proportion, and the golden section, a magical, infinite number (1.618) represented by the Greek letter PHI ϕ, which will be explored in detail in a later chapter.

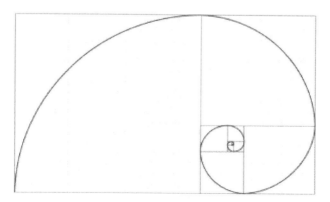

Fibonacci Spiral Generated from PHI

The expansion of the universe can be thought of as a masculine process of dispersion in a hyper-dimensional fractal cube-like fashion and the formation of matter through a process of contraction, densification & cohesion can be thought of as feminine. The very act of creation is fundamentally a feminine transmutation process of primordial substance into constructs.

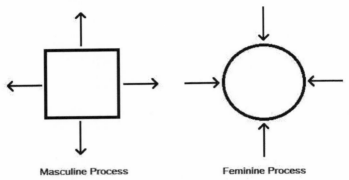

Masculine Process   **Feminine Process**

As mentioned earlier, this spiral of creation is the core of inspiration which the Merriam-Webster dictionary defines as:

- A Divine influence or action on a person believed to qualify him or her to receive and communicate sacred revelation
- The action or power of moving the intellect or emotions
- The act of influencing or suggesting opinions
- The act of drawing in; *specifically*: the drawing of air into the lungs
- The quality or state of being inspired
- Something that is inspired: *A scheme that was pure inspiration*
- An inspiring agent or influence

Gurdjieff said that before examining the laws of transformation of Unity into Plurality we have to examine the fundamental law that creates all phenomena in all the diversity or unity of all universes, which he dubbed the 'Law of Three', or the law of the *three principles* or *three forces*, and that every phenomenon on whatever scale and in whatever world it takes place, from molecular to cosmic, was the result of the combination or meeting of three different and opposing forces.

The first force was called active or positive, the second, passive or negative, and the third, neutralizing.

The creation of a permanent third principle is for man the transformation of duality into trinity and can be clearly seen in the permutation of duality and the basis of the expression of life, when the circle that encompasses "all that is" moves in a primary scission that divides itself into what is termed the Vescica Pisces. In this dualistic split, 1 into 2 instantly becomes 3.

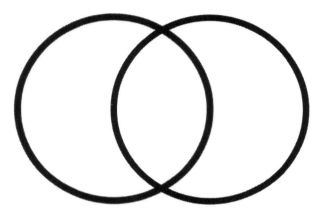

Vescica Pisces

Our conscious awareness lives in this middle ground that represents the focal point, infinity zone, and fulcrum between subjectivity and objectivity or spirit and matter, and we have a front row seat where we control the interpretation and what we choose to manifest as a result of that stimuli. This is a zero point, ground zero, the eye of the storm, and the center of the universe, which is *nothing* - a place of power.

In the earliest traditions the supreme being was represented by a sphere, the symbol of a being with no beginning, no end, continually existing, perfectly formed, and profoundly symmetrical. The addition of a second sphere represented the expansion of unity into the duality of male and female, god and goddess. By overlapping, the two spheres, the god and goddess created a divine offspring.

The Vesica Pisces motif and its derivatives, the Flower of Life, Tree of Life, and fundamentals of geometry have a history of thousands of years and easily predates virtually all major religions of the current era.

The son or daughter of the god and goddess is associated with the overlapping of the spheres. In the case of Jesus Christ, the two dimensional figure also served as a symbol for the miracle of the fishes. The "tail" also served to more easily identify the source of the plane figure. There is also conveyed the spiritual power originating from the interior of this symbol.

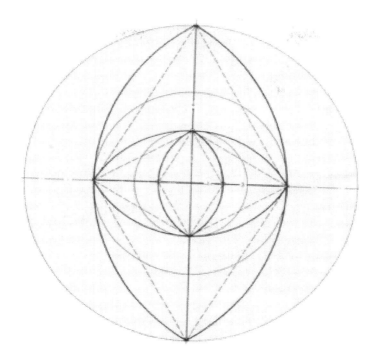

The intersection of two overlapping spheres, including their interior portion, and/or the more common two dimensional version represents among other things:

- The joining of God and Goddess to create an offspring
- A symbol for Jesus Christ
- In art a pointed oval used as an n aureole in medieval sculpture and painting
- The vagina of the female goddess
- The basic motif in the Flower of Life
- An overlay of the Tree of Life
- The formative power of polygons
- A geometrical description of square roots and harmonic proportions
- 7) A source of immense power and energy

Virtually every medieval church in Europe uses as a standard motif of the Vesica Pisces in two dimensions. The fact that many of these churches were dedicated to the Virgin Mary or to Mary Madagalene (aka the goddess) is simply part of the understanding. Several of the churches in northern France are even located in such a manner that their *points of light* recreate the "lights" of the constellation Virgo. In Glastonbury, England, the site normally attributed to Avalon (the island of the Goddess), is also where the Chapel of St. Mary is located -- the latter which is apparently patterned with the use of the Vesica Pisces.

The goddess of any and all religions which recognize her power and significance invariably use the Vesica Pisces to identify her. From the overlapping pools of water and the chalice well cover in the goddess's garden in Glastonbury to any number of representations of the Tree of Life, the goddess and her ability to create and birth life are celebrated.

Drunvalo Melchizedek, in his Flower of Life symbolism, uses the Vesica Pisces and considers it the geometric image through which light was created.

Flower of Life

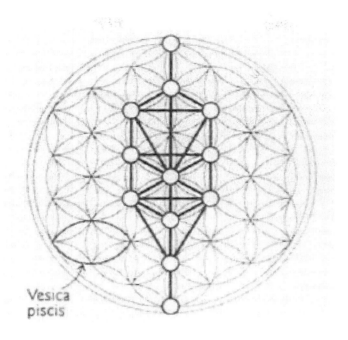

Vesica
piscis

Tree of Life

The Tree of Life is shown here in one of its many representations and includes the Vesica Pisces and Flower of Life. The ease with which the patterns fit make the inclusion virtually automatic.

Robert Lawlor, in *Sacred Geometry: Philosophy & Practice,* one of the best books available on Sacred Geometry notes that the Ö3 contained within the Vesica Pisces is "the formative power giving rise to the polygonal 'world'."

Additionally, the square roots of 2, 3, and 5 (three of the first digits in the Fibonacci Numbers) can be geometrically calculated. This is just an inkling of the possibilities and relationships that can be explored.

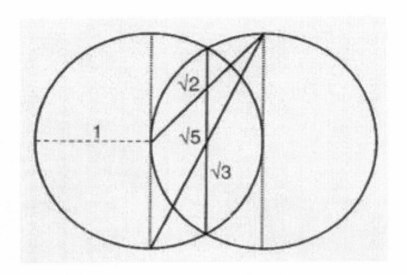

GURDJIEFF'S INFINITE OCTAVE

The number "8" tilted on its side represents the octave of infinity. Among other things its form applies its dynamics back and forth through the inner spectrum of cognition across the boundaries of thought and matter and back again, from the mental to the physical; to the depths of infinity inside of us, to the boundless infinity without.

In order to navigate the physical world our senses take in a multitude of stimuli and what our senses take in our minds process continuously, reinterpreting the incoming data from moment to moment, instantaneously making adjustments to a shifting environment. By regulating our breathing, heartbeat, and blood pressure, as well as other unconscious physiological functions, our body's natural intelligence strives for balance; especially when it is involved in intense physical activity requiring great coordination, like sports or dancing.

This rapid exchange between inner subjectivity and outer objectivity is an infinity pattern between external stimulus and inner interpretation and the continuous volley and serve of stimulus and response moves back and forth in the same manner as a tennis match, only this match is played at very high speed with multiple volleys.

Not only is this a rapid subjective objective dance, but the two sides of the brain also communicate on many levels, instantaneously sending masses of information volleying back and forth across the "net" of the corpus callosum, the central area in the fissure of the brain that facilitates communication between both sides.

This same principle applies when we consider how a pendulum swings down and moves at its greatest speed when it passes the middle point and goes slower and slower as it rises on the other side until it reverses its movement. The greatest amount of energy is at the center as opposed to the extremes where the power is the weakest. In the same manner, the greatest power in our solar system lies in the sun that resides at its center. If you study terrestrial energy manifestations like hurricanes, one of the most powerful forces of nature, it revolves around the eye of the storm, its calmest place and its center of power.

In our dualistic world view we tend to focus on the extremes, falsely believing them to be the places of maximum power, but the greatest power always resides in the center where we transcend the opposites, understanding that it is not the polarities that deserve our attention, it is the energy in between; the infinity zone.

The mathematical symbol that represents the three dimensional form and fourth dimensional motion is a sideways figure 8 - ∞ , and the central point of the infinity symbol where transition occurs represents the center where the greatest power lies.

It is no accident that tremendous power has been attributed to the number 8, which has great meaning and significance throughout history and cultures worldwide. In numerology it is considered the most powerful of all numbers.

8 is the base figure of the octal number system and has been the axis around which number systems evolved across the globe. The most commonly used decimal system can be chronologically traced back to the octal system, adding more substance to the belief that 8 is the number of regeneration and new life.

The properties, qualities, and beliefs around 8 are endless. Its multitude of attributes have been culled to give examples from the many realms that it influences.

In mathematics:

- 8 is a composite number, its proper divisors being 1, 2, and 4. It is twice 4 or four times 2. Eight is a power of two being 2^3.
- The Prime Factors of 8=2x2x2.
- 8 is the base of the octal number system, which is mostly used with computers. In octal, one digit represents 3 bits. In modern computers, a byte is a grouping of eight bits, also called an octet.
- 8 is the largest cube in the Fibonacci Sequence, being 3 plus 5. The next Fibonacci number is 13. 8 is the only positive Fibonacci number, aside from 1, that is a perfect cube.
- The maximal number of regions into which a plane can be divided by 3 circles = 8
- 8 is the maximal number of regions into which space can be divided by 3 Spheres.
- A polygon with eight sides is an octagon.
- Figurate numbers representing octagons (including eight) are called octagonal numbers. A polyhedron with eight faces is an octahedron. A cuboctahedron has as faces six equal squares and eight equal regular triangles.
- A Truncated Tetrahedron is an Archimedean Solid with 8 Faces. It has four triangles and four hexagons.
- The Cube is a Platonic Solid with 8 Vertices.
- Sphenic numbers always have exactly eight divisors.
- A figure 8 is the common name of a geometric shape, often used in the context of sports, such as skating. Figure-eight turns of a rope or cable around a cleat, pin, or bitt are used to belay something.

In Physics:

- In nuclear physics 8 is the second magic number.
- In particle physics the eightfold way is used to classify sub-atomic particles.

In Astronomy:

- As of 2006, in our Solar System, eight of the bodies orbiting the Sun are considered to be planets.

In Chemistry:

- The atomic number of oxygen.
- The number of allotropes of carbon.
- The most stable allotrope of a sulphur molecule is made of eight sulphur atoms arranged in a rhombic form.
- The maximum number of electrons that can occupy a valence shell.

In Biology:

- All spiders, and more generally all arachnids, have eight legs. Orb-weaver spiders of the cosmopolitan family Areneidae have eight similar eyes.
- The octopus and its cephalopod relatives in genus Argonauta have eight arms (tentacles).

In General:

- Timothy Leary identified a hierarchy of eight levels of consciousness.
- In human adult dentition there are eight teeth in each quadrant. The eighth tooth is the so-called wisdom tooth.
- There are eight cervical nerves on each side in man and most mammals.

- In chess, each side has eight pawns and the board is made of 64 squares arranged in an eight by eight lattice. The eight queens puzzle is a challenge to arrange eight queens on the board so that none can capture any of the others.

According to the Richard Phillips web site:

- Eight is the third number that stays the same when written upside down.
- Scorpions have eight legs.
- According to Indian mythology, the Earth is supported on the backs of eight white elephants.
- Before the rise of Christianity, there were eight days in the Greek and Roman weeks.
- Many words beginning *oct-* are related to the number eight. An octopus has eight arms and an octet is a group of eight musicians.
- An octagon is a figure with eight sides and an octahedron has eight faces.

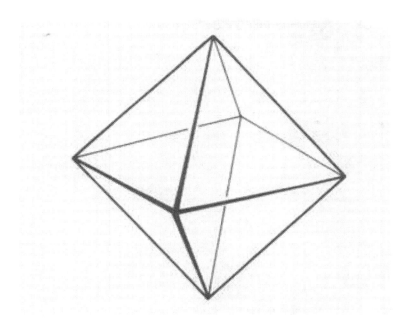

Eight triangular faces on an octahedron.

1 x **8** + 1 = 9
12 x **8** + 2 = 98
123 x **8** + 3 = 987
1 234 x **8** + 4 = 9 876
12 345 x **8** + 5 = 98 765
123 456 x **8** + 6 = 987 654
1 234 567 x **8** + 7 = 9 876 543
12 345 678 x **8** + 8 = 98 765 432
123 456 789 x **8** + 9 = 987 654 321

According to the Riding the Beast web site, the number 8 has the following properties:

Symbolism:

- Number of the perfection, the infinity. In mathematics the symbol of the infinity is represented by a 8 laid down.
- Symbol of the cosmic Christ.
- Number figuring the immutable eternity or the self-destruction. It represents also the final point of the manifestation.
- In China, 8 expresses the totality of the universe.
- Number of the balance and of the cosmic order, according to the Egyptians.
- Number expressing matter, it is also the symbol of the incarnation in matter which becomes itself creative and autonomous, governing its own laws.
- The number eight corresponds to the New Testament, according to Ambroise.
- It is the symbol of the new Life, the final Resurrection and the anticipated Resurrection that is the baptism.
- According to Clement of Alexandria, the Christ places under the sign of 8 the one he made to be born again.
- Represent the totality and the coherence of the creation in evolution. In China, it expresses the totality of the universe.
- Represent the earth, not in its surface but in its volume, since 8 is the first cubic number.

- The Pythagoreans have made the number 8 the symbol of love and friendship, prudence and thinking. They called it the Great "Tetrachtys".
- In Babylon, Egypt, and Arabia, it was the number of the duplication devoted to the sun, from where the solar disc is decorated with a cross of eight arms.
- The number 8 means multiplicity for the Japanese.
- A favorable number, associated to the prosperity.
- It is the number of the restful day, after the 7th day of the creation.

General:

- Eight is the total number of Chakras of the man, counting the seven in correlation with the physical body, plus an additional working in the etheric body. This eighth Chakra is known as "the Chakra of the Soul" or "the Star Chakra", located approximately 7 to 10 centimeters above the Crown Chakra.
- The eight great gods of the Vedas: Surya, Candra, Agni, Yama, Varuna, Indra, Vâyu and Kubera.
- The eight "trigrams" of "Fou-Hi" Chinese philosopher.

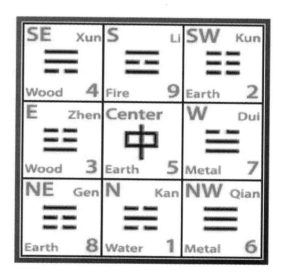

- The eight parts of the way which leads to the nirvana, according to the Buddhist doctrines: the faith, the right judgement, the right language, a right and pure action, a right profession, the application of the spirit to all the precepts of the law, the right memory and the right meditation.
- The Buddhists count eight symbols of long life of which one of them is the infinite node being rolled up and withdrawn on itself.
- There are eight degrees of Buddhist monks or "Aryas" and the highest is named "Arhat".
- According to a Buddhist legend, Buddha's ashes were separated in eight parts.
- The lotus is represented symbolically with 8 petals and according to yogis, it is on a lotus with 8 petals that the "Mêru" mount is erected which, symbolically, represents the center and the axis of the world.
- Yoga counts eight training courses: Yama, the restriction; Niyama, religious observances; Asana, the posture; Pranayama, the control of the breathing; Praty-ahara, the restriction of senses; Dharana, the concentration; Dhyana, the contemplation and Samadhi, the ecstasy.
- The number eight governs the life of man: at 8 month the baby teeth appear; at 8 years, he loses them; at 2 x 8 years, it is puberty; and he becomes impotent at 8 x 8 years.

From the Mystical numbers web site:

- **Eight symbolizes the ability to make decisions**.
- **Eight symbolizes abundance and power.**
- The Pythagoreans called the number eight "Ogdoad" and considered it the "**little holy number**".
- In China eight is homonym for prosperity. When pronounced it sounds much like the word "prosper".
- **A double eight**, as in 88, is said to **bring double joy**.
- The eighth **day of the Chinese New Year** is the day for the annual gathering of all the gods in Heaven.
- In the Tarot, eight is the card for Justice or Strength.
- The stop sign has eight sides.

- It takes **eight minutes** for the sun's light to reach the earth.
- In Ancient Rome the eighth day was an important day to a newborn child. If the newborn lived to the eighth day the child was worth special attention. On this day the baby was rubbed with salt for protection against evil spirits.
- Hinduism - The Star of Lakshmi. Lakshmi is the Hindu goddess of Wealth. The Star of Lakshmi is the eight pointed star made up of two squares. The points symbolize the eight kinds of wealth provided by Lakshmi.

From a mythological perspective, Apollo 8, the second crewed mission in the American Apollo space program was the first human spaceflight to leave Earth orbit; the first to be captured by and escape from the gravitational field of another celestial body; and the first crewed voyage to return to Earth from another celestial body — Earth's Moon.

These milestones are the most significant and literally the farthest reaching, most powerful accomplishments of modern man.

According to The Numbers and Their Meanings blogspot, the number 8:

Resolves dualities, expansion, dissolution, dimension of the timeless, good and bad, right and wrong, day and night, the ability to see and relate to eternal dimensions, balance between forces, connects spirit and matter, developing confidence to follow a vision, breaks down barriers to transformation, reality, and courage.

All of these qualities transcend duality and bridge realities, manifesting tremendous power by resolving the paradox of opposites in a transformation from two into one.

Because the number 8 symbolizes power, it is shifted ninety degrees to symbolize infinity, ∞ to refer to something *without any limit*. It is a concept that is relevant in a number of fields, predominantly mathematics and physics. Having a recognizable history in these disciplines reaching back into the time of ancient Greek civilization, the term in the English language derives from Latin *infinitas*, which is translated as "unboundedness".

In mathematics, "infinity" is often treated as a number, but it is not the same kind of number as real numbers. In number systems incorporating infinitesimals, the reciprocal of an infinitesimal is an infinite number, i.e. a number greater than any real number.

The mathematical symbol for infinity is called the lemniscate and the infinity sign was devised in 1655 by mathematician John Wallis, and named lemniscus (latin, ribbon) by mathematician Bernoulli about forty years later. The lemniscate is patterned after the device known as a Mobius, named after a nineteenth century mathematician Mobius.

A mobius strip is a strip of paper that is twisted and attached at the ends, forming an 'endless' two dimensional surface. The religious aspect of the infinity symbol predates its mathematical origins. Similar symbols have been found in Tibetan rock carvings; and the ouroboros, or infinity snake, is often depicted in this shape. In the tarot it represents the balance of forces and is often associated with the magician card.

Ancient cultures had numerous ideas about the nature of infinity. The ancient Indians and Greeks, unable to codify infinity in terms of a formalized mathematical system approached it as a philosophical concept.

THE INFINITE OCTAVE IN ART AND MUSIC

Art and music reflect our inner life, appealing to our innate sense of beauty, inspired by the natural world around us. The geometries present in these disciplines are an integral part of what we perceive as beauty. We recognize the grace of these relationships in nature and mimic their perfection visually in the static arts of painting and photography, and in the dynamic arts of film, dance, and other forms of movement, as well as the auditory bliss of inspired music.

In ancient Greece mathematical disciplines introduced in childhood combined gymnastics and music until age 17 or 18, emphasizing gymnastics until the age of 20. This training was designed to stabilize the equilibrium of the soul, viewed by Plato as straddling the upper Intelligible realm and the lower Sensible realm so the individual could recognize the symmetry and harmony common to both music and bodily movement. The intention was for the equilibrium established in the souls of individuals to be reflected in the harmony of the State.

In Egyptian belly dancing a figure 8 with hips is comprised of two different isolations, the hip slide and the twist. The belly dance reverse figure 8 move is called the Turkish figure 8 which requires the dancers to pull in towards the center.

Contra dance choreography specifies the dance formation known as the *figures* and the sequence of those figures in a dance. The figures usually repeat a consistent pattern aligned with the phrasing of the music. A figure is a pattern of movement that typically takes eight counts, although figures with four or sixteen counts are common. Each dance is a collection of figures assembled to allow the dancers to progress along the set. A contra dance is typically 64 counts with a 32-measure tune.

To get the most effective rim shot on a snare drum, the swing of the arm and the wrist flex upward in a bend, making the first half of a figure 8, then down, snapping the wrist in a whip like action in the second half, catching the rim and the head of the drum simultaneously, resulting in a powerful "crack" sound.

Choreographed movements in time and space like those associated with dance and music multiply and enhance the left and right brain informational volleys across the "net" of the corpus callosum. This process is highly active in drumming as described in *The Healing Power of the Drum* by Robert Lawrence Friedman.

"One of the most powerful aspects of drumming and the reason that people have done it since the beginning of being human is that it changes people's consciousness. Through rhythmic repetition of ritual sounds, the body, brain and the nervous system are energized and transformed. When a group of people play a rhythm for an extended period of time, their brain waves become entrained to the rhythm and they have a shared brain wave state. The longer the drumming goes on, the more powerful the entrainment becomes. It's really the oldest holy communion. All of the oldest known religious rites used drumming as part of the shared religious experience."

It is interesting to study drumming from the perspective of scientific research into the functioning of the brain. Using electroencephalographs, scientists can measure the number of energy waves per second pulsing through the brain. A system of classifying states of consciousness according to the frequencies of these waves was created.

Normal outwardly focused attention generates beta waves that vibrate from 14 to 40 cycles per second. When awareness shifts to an internal focus, our brain slows down into the more rhythmical waves of alpha at 7-14 waves per second. As discussed earlier alpha is defined by relaxation and centering. Dropping down to 4-7 cycles per second the brain enters the theta state where there is an interfacing of conscious and unconscious processes, producing hypnologic dream-like imagery at the threshold of sleep. Theta is the course of sudden mystical insights and creative solutions to complex situations and is marked by physical and emotional healing. People with a preponderance of theta brainwaves are also able to learn and process much more information than normal.

The brain is divided into two hemispheres that are split in their control of the thinking process. The right brain functions as the creative, visual, aural and emotional center and the left brain is the rational, logical, analytical and verbal administrator. Generally, either the right or left brain dominates in cycles lasting from 30 minutes to 3 hours. While one hemisphere is dominant, the memories, skills, and information of the other hemisphere are less available, residing in a subconscious or unconscious realm.

Not only do the right and left brain operate in different modes, they usually operate in different brain wave rhythms. The right brain may be generating alpha waves while the left brain is in the beta state, or both can generate the same type of brain waves while remaining out of sync with each other. In states of intense creativity, deep meditation or under the influence of rhythmic sound, both hemispheres can become entrained to the same rhythm. This state of unified whole brain functioning is called hemispheric synchronization or the awakened mind.

Music appeals to our sense of beauty through sound that expresses infinity in time. We appreciate the beauty of music when the musician has mastered the use of octaves, sound, timing, silences, and the universal mathematical laws inherent in its structure. Its appeal is universal.

Pythagoras is often credited for discovering that an oscillating string stopped halfway along its length produces an octave relative to the string's fundamental, while a ratio of 2:3 produces a perfect fifth and 3:4 produces a perfect fourth, but the Chinese had instruments that were thousands of years older, such as the Guqin, that also feature these tonal scales.

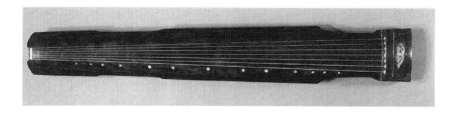

Pythagoreans believed that these harmonic ratios gave music powers of healing which could "harmonize" an out-of-balance body.

This belief has been revived with the proliferation of sound healers in modern times.

In Music:

- A note played for one-eighth the duration of a whole note is called an eighth note, or quaver.
- An octave, the interval between two notes with the same letter name (where one has double the frequency of the other), is so called because there are eight notes between the two on a standard major or minor diatonic scale, including the notes themselves, which are without chromatic deviation. The ecclesiastical modes are ascending diatonic musical scales of eight notes or tones comprising an octave.
- There are eight notes in the octatonic scale.
- There are eight musicians in a double quartet or an octet. Both terms may also refer to a musical composition for eight voices or instruments.

An octave is the interval in music between two notes where the higher note has twice the frequency of the lower. On a piano keyboard this corresponds to an interval of eight white notes, for example, the notes C D E F G A B C.

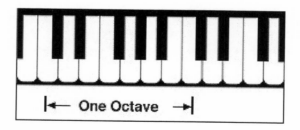

A musical scale sounds incomplete unless you play all eight notes, which is why there are eight notes rather than seven in an octave. The term *octave* belongs to Western music, but the musical interval occurs in music around the world.

Harmony is the use of simultaneous pitches, tones, notes, or chords. The study of harmony involves chords, their construction, and chord progressions and the principles of connection that govern them. Harmony is said to refer to the "vertical" aspect of music as distinguished from melodic line, or "horizontal" aspect. Counterpoint refers to the interweaving of melodic lines, and polyphony refers to the relationship of separate independent voices. They are sometimes distinguished from harmony.

In popular and jazz harmony chords are named by their root plus various terms and characters indicating their qualities. In many types of music, notably baroque, romantic, modern, and jazz, chords are augmented with "tensions", additional chord members that create a dissonant interval in relation to the bass. Typically, in the classical Common practice period a dissonant chord will "resolve" to a consonant chord. Harmonization sounds pleasant to the ear when there is a balance between the consonant and dissonant sounds and it occurs when there is a balance between "tense" and "relaxed" moments.

This concept known as relaxed tension is the central point where energy is mastered in balance. Every high level tennis player, drummer, dancer, or athlete knows the effortlessness of this center of power and control. Musica universalis, known as universal music, or music of the spheres, is an ancient philosophical concept that regards proportions in the movements of celestial bodies; the Sun, Moon, and planets as a form of musica, the Medieval Latin name for music. This 'music' is not usually thought to be literally audible, but a harmonic and/or mathematical and/or religious concept. The idea appealed to musical thinkers until the end of the Renaissance, influencing scholars of many kinds, including humanists.

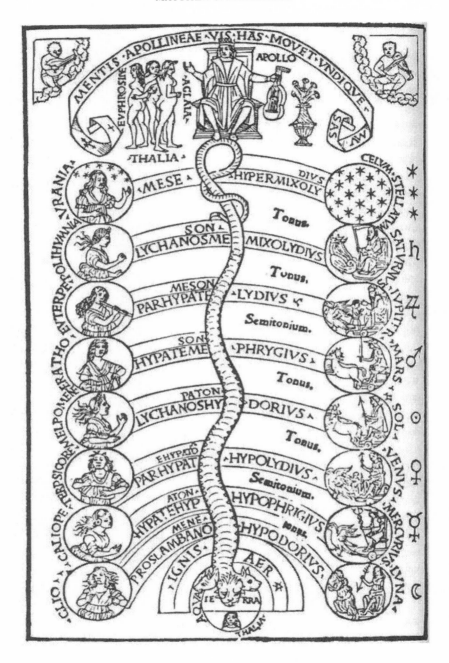

Engraving from Renaissance Italy showing Apollo, the Muses, the planetary spheres, and musical ratios.

The Music of the Spheres incorporates the metaphysical principle that mathematical relationships express qualities or 'tones' of energy that manifest in numbers, visual angles, shapes and sounds, all connected within a pattern of proportion. Pythagoras first identified that the pitch of a musical note is in proportion to the length of the string that produces it, and that intervals between harmonious sound frequencies form simple numerical ratios.

In a theory known as the Harmony of the Spheres, Pythagoras proposed that the sun, moon, and planets all emit their own unique hum known as orbital resonance, based on their orbital revolution, and that the quality of life on Earth reflects the tenor of celestial sounds that are imperceptible to the human ear. Subsequently, Plato described astronomy and music as "twinned" studies of sensual recognition: astronomy for the eyes and music for the ears, both requiring knowledge of numerical proportions.

Later philosophers kept the close association between astronomy, optics, music, and astrology, including Ptolemy, who wrote influential texts on these topics. Alkindi, in the 9th century, developed Ptolemy's ideas in *De Aspectibus* which explores many points of relevance to astrology and the use of planetary aspects.

In the 17th century, Johannes Kepler influenced by arguments in Ptolemy's *Tetrabiblos, Optics and Harmonica,* compiled his Harmonices Mundi, 'Harmony of the World', that presented his own analysis of optical perceptions, geometrical shapes, musical consonances, and planetary harmonies. According to Kepler, all the connections that exist between sacred geometry, cosmology, astrology, harmonics, and music are all through *musica universalis*. Kepler regarded this text as the most important work of his career, and the fifth part, concerning the role of planetary harmony in creation, the crown of it. His premise was that, as an integral part of Universal Law, mathematical harmony is the key that binds all parts together. One theoretical proposition from his work introduced the minor planetary aspects and harmonics into astrology, another introduced Kepler's third law of planetary motion into astronomy.

The three branches of the Medieval concept of musica were presented by Boethius in his book *De Musica*:

- *musica mundana*; sometimes referred to as ***musica universalis***
- *musica humana*; the internal music of the human body

- *musica quae in quibusdam constituta est instrumentis;* sounds made by singers and instrumentalists

According to Max Heindel's Rosicrucian writings, the heavenly "music of the spheres" is heard in the *Region of Concrete Thought*, the lower region of the mental plane, which is an ocean of harmony. It is also referred to in Esoteric Christianity as the place where the state of consciousness known as the "Second Heaven" occurs.

When this universal order is embraced, the infinite realms that we see outside of ourselves are reflected in the infinite realms inside of us, and the polar aspects of the infinity zone come into resonance, making us one in universal harmony.

This is what it means to be empowered.

THE EXPRESSION OF THE SACRED IN GEOMETRY

Sacred geometry is used in the planning and construction of religious structures like churches, temples, mosques, and other religious monuments, altars, and tabernacles as well as sacred spaces like sacred groves, village greens, holy wells, and in the creation of religious art.

In sacred geometry symbolic and sacred meanings are ascribed to certain geometric shapes and proportions. In the ancient world certain numbers had symbolic meaning aside from their ordinary use for counting or calculating. Plane figures, polygons, triangles, squares, hexagons, and so forth were related to numbers in the same manner as the number three is to the triangle. Because they were visual they carried more emotional value than the numbers themselves.

The belief that God created the universe according to a geometric plan has ancient origins. Plutarch attributed the belief to Plato, writing "Plato said God geometrizes continually".

The study of sacred geometry has its roots in the study of nature and the mathematical principles at work there. Many natural forms can be related to geometry, such as the chambered nautilus that grows at a constant rate. Its shell forms a logarithmic spiral to accommodate that growth without changing shape.

Honeybees construct hexagonal cells to hold their honey and the bumblebee compound eye is formed of a large number of individual hexagonal units called ommatidia. These and other correspondences in nature provide further proof of the cosmic significance of geometric forms, all of which can be explained through natural principles.

Honeycomb

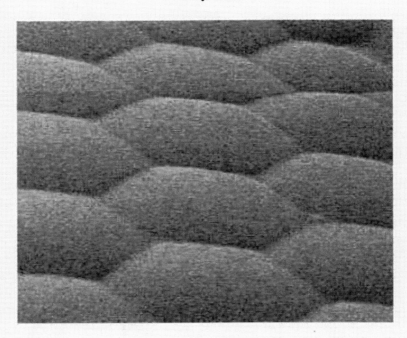

Bumblebee eye showing individual ommatidia

Passion Flower

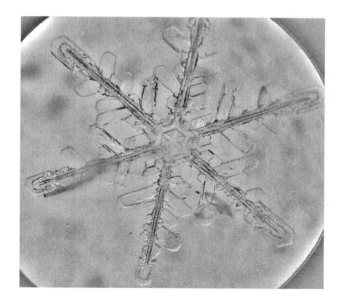

Snowflake

The golden ratio or divine proportion, geometric ratios, and geometric figures were often employed in the design of Egyptian, ancient Indian, Greek, and Roman architecture. Medieval European cathedrals also incorporated symbolic geometry. Indian and Himalayan spiritual communities constructed temples and fortifications on design plans of the mandala and yantra.

In philosophy, especially that of Aristotle, the golden mean is the desirable middle between two extremes, one of excess and the other of deficiency. As an example courage, a virtue, if taken to excess would manifest as recklessness, and if found to be deficient as cowardice.

To Greek mentality it was an attribute of beauty. Both ancients and moderns realized a close association in mathematics between beauty and truth. The Greeks believed there to be three ingredients to beauty: symmetry, proportion, and harmony. This triad of principles infused their life. They were attuned to beauty as an object of love and something to be imitated and reproduced in their lives, architecture, education, and politics. They judged life by this mentality.

In Chinese philosophy, a similar concept, Doctrine of the Mean, was propounded by Confucius. Buddhist philosophy also includes the concept of the middle way.

The Golden Ratio lies at the core of sacred geometry. Also known as the Golden Cut, the Golden Rectangle, The Divine Proportion, and other names, the Golden Mean, like PI 3.14) is another of those strange numbers that we seldom question and often take for granted. This magical, infinite number (1.618) is represented by the Greek letter PHI φ. Different from PI, the golden mean goes unnoticed in our everyday life in such things as buildings, plants, and living creatures, yet we find these things strangely pleasing to the eye.

The ancient mathematician Fibonacci discovered that if you start with the numbers 0 and 1 and add them together you get a new number -- in this case 1. If you add the last number and the new number together, you get another new number, 2. If you keep doing this, you end up with a long list of unique numbers known as the Fibonacci Series.

0, 1 -- Added together gives a new number 1.
0, 1, 1 -- Add the last two numbers and new number is 2.
0, 1, 1, 1, 2 -- Add the last two numbers and the new number is 3.
0, 1, 1, 2, 3 -- Add the last two numbers and the new number is 5.
0,1,1,2,3,5
The additions grow into a series of unique numbers.
0,1,1,2,3,5,8,13,21,34,55,89,144, 233,377 to infinity.

Starting from zero, if you take any two SEQUENTIAL numbers and calculate the ratio between them, an interesting pattern emerges.

1,0	Ratio	=	1	to	0	=	0
1,1	Ratio	=	1	to	1	=	1
2,1	Ratio	=	2	to	1	=	2
3,2	Ratio	=	3	to	2	=	1.5
5,3 Ratio		=	5	to	3	=	1.6666
8,5	Ratio	=	8	to	5	=	1.6
13,8 Ratio		=	13	to	8	=	1.625
21,13 Ratio		=	21	to13		=	1.61538
34,21 Ratio		=	34	to	21	=	1.61538
55,34 Ratio		=	55	to	34	=	1.61764
89,55 Ratio		=	89	to	55	=	1.6181

144,89 Ratio = 144 to 89 = 1.6179

If you continue in this manner the decimal figure will revolve around the magic number 1.618 because it is an infinite number.

Here is an example of how the golden mean occurs in nature. The diagram below is made up of squares, but the overall image is a rectangle that has the magic ratio of 1.618. The curved lines within each of the squares are quarter circles, but as a whole they look like the cross section of a sea shell. This is in fact the same as the growth rate of the beautiful Nautilus Sea Shell - i.e. 1.618, and as discussed earlier, is a combination of the interacting angled masculine and the curved feminine.

Cutaway of a Chambered Nautilus

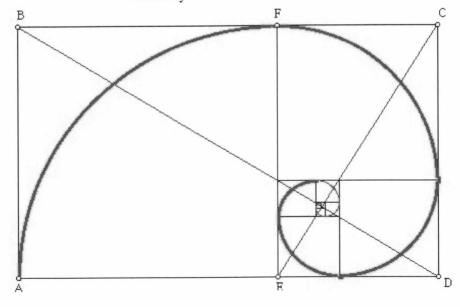

Another interesting phenomenon of the Fibonacci sequence and the golden mean within nature is the sunflower. If you count the spirals, there are 55 with either 34 or 89 on either side going in a counter clockwise direction which is a Fibonacci sequence. If a Fibonacci number is divided by its immediate predecessor in the sequence, the quotient approximates the golden mean.

Sunflower

Other examples abound on both microcosmic and macrocosmic scales.

Fractals in a Romanesco broccoli.

A low pressure area shows an approximately logarithmic spiral pattern.

The arms of spiral galaxies often have the shape of logarithmic spirals, like those shown here in the Whirlpool Galaxy.

Contemporary use of the term *sacred geometry* describes assertions of a mathematical order to the intrinsic nature of the universe. Scientists see the same geometric and mathematical patterns arising from natural principles.

Aside from the golden spiral, among the most prevalent traditional geometric forms ascribed to sacred geometry are:

The sine wave:

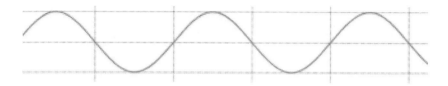

The sphere:

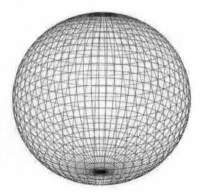

The vesica piscis:

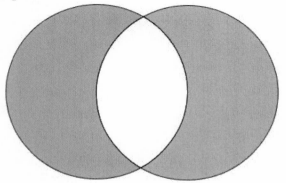

The torus:

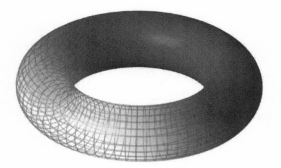

The 5 platonic solids:

| Tetrahedron (four faces) | Cube or hexahedron (six faces) | Octahedron (eight faces) | Dodecahedron (twelve faces) | Icosahedron (twenty faces) |

The tesseract (4-dimensional cube):

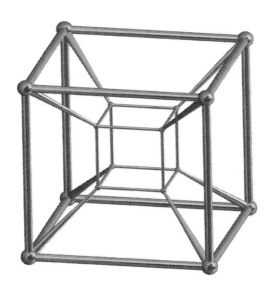

Fractals:

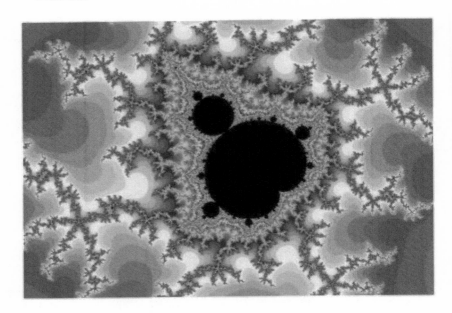

Star tetrahedron:

Many of the sacred geometric principles of the human body and ancient architecture have been compiled into the well-known Vitruvian Man drawing by Leonardo Da Vinci, based on the much older writings of the Roman architect Vitruvius.

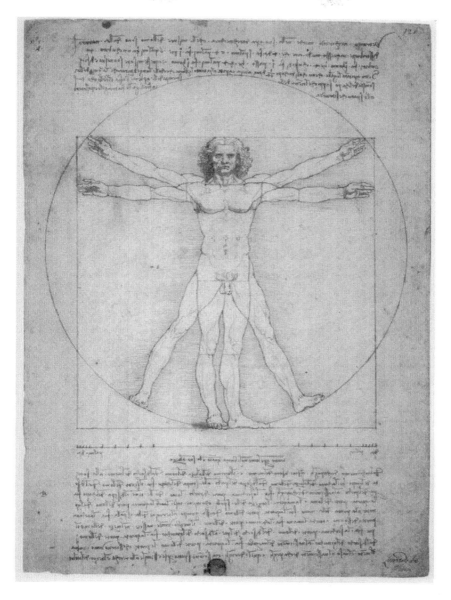

The Vitruvian Man

THE EXPRESSION OF THE SACRED IN MAN

The geometric principles of the human body and ancient architecture were recorded long before the Roman architect Vitruvius and Da Vinci came up with their now famous drawing.

Ancient wisdom from many cultures tells us that our body is our temple. One of the most profound, densely packed storehouses of wisdom known to man is contained in the temple of Amun-Mut-Khonsu in Egypt. This Temple of Anthropocosmic Man at Luxor is a masterpiece of art, science, and spirituality laid out in an elegant structure that is architecturally rendered to exhibit within its design and artwork the same proportions as the proportions of Man, as well as the mathematical and geometrical structure of the Cosmos and its locale within human consciousness. Pharaonic Consciousness not only recognized Man as the center of the Universe, it could formally equate it as well.

In his smaller work, "The Temple *in* Man", that distills the massive two volume set "The Temple *of* Man", R. A. Schwaller de Lubicz shares his observations of the temple.

"...the canon proportions of the profile and the head, and of the head in relation to the body, are present. Here the Golden Number comes to our aid. It controls all vegetable and animal growth... The outline of a human skeleton—traced according to anthropometrical methods and very carefully constructed, bone by bone—was superimposed on the general plan of the temple. The head (full face for the skeleton) is located exactly in the sanctuaries of the covered temple; the sanctuary of the barque of

Amun is in the oral cavity; the clavicles are marked by walls; the chest is located in the first hypostyle of the covered temple and ends with the temple's platform. The abdomen is represented by the peristyle court, and the pubis is located exactly at the door separating this peristyle from the colonnade of Amun.

This marvelous colonnade is, in fact, dedicated to the femurs, the thighs; the knees are at the site of the gate in front of which sit the two colossi, marking the entrance to this colonnade. The tibias are in the court of Ramses, framed by the colossi, whose legs (tibias) are particularly pronounced. The little toe of our skeleton falls exactly at the northwest angle of the pylon. One might be tempted to think this skeleton had been constructed to be superimposed on the temple. But any skeleton, as long as it is harmonious (like the one represented here) can be projected thus on the plan of the temple and will coincide with it. Moreover, all the proportions of the skeleton may be checked against the actual measurements of the temple.

For my report, it was necessary to have recourse to the Egyptian canon; I have in this regard devoted a chapter to a subject that has never been dealt with until now—the importance the Ancients accorded the crown of the skull (cava).

This crown of the skull, marked off in Egyptian figuration by a headband, a diadem, a headdress or crown—is a veritable revelation with regard to psycho-spiritual knowledge of the Ancients.

This is made clear by the placement of the principal organs of the Intellect and of all the control mechanisms of life in the various sanctuaries, whose figurations, texts, and architecture specify their purpose.

The Temple of Luxor is indisputably devoted to the Human Microcosm. This consecration is not merely a simple attribution: the entire temple becomes a book explaining the secret functions of the organs and nerve centers."

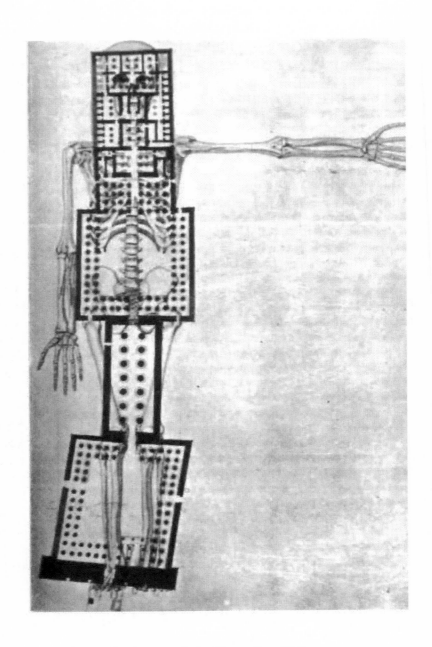

Diagram of the Temple of Man

The human body is phi-designed as the golden section template seen throughout our whole human form ratios, proving that humans like the macrocosm of the planets and stars, and the microcosm of atomic and subatomic particles were all created using the PHI design.

The first example of the golden ratio in the average human body is when the distance between the navel and the foot is taken as 1 unit, the height of a human being is equivalent to 1.618.

Some other golden proportions in the average human body are:

The distance between the finger tip and the elbow and the distance between the wrist and the elbow.

The distance between the shoulder line and the top of the head and the head length.

The distance between the navel and the top of the head and the distance between the shoulder line and the top of the head.

The distance between the navel and knee and the distance between the knee and the end of the foot.

Our fingers have three sections. The proportion of the first two to the full length of the finger gives the golden ratio, with the exception of the thumbs. The proportion of the middle finger to the little finger is also a golden ratio. We have two hands, and the fingers on them consist of three sections. There are five fingers on each hand. Only eight of these are articulated according to the golden number: 2, 3, 5, and 8 which fit the Fibonacci numbers.

Likewise, there are several golden ratios in the human face.

The total width of the two front teeth in the upper jaw over their height gives a golden ratio. The width of the first tooth from the centre to the second tooth also yields the golden ratio of 1.618. These are the ideal proportions that a dentist may consider. Some other golden ratios in the human face are:

Length of the face to the width of the face.

The distance between the lips and where the eyebrows meet and the length of the nose.

The length of the face and the distance between the tip of jaw and where the eyebrows meet.

The length of the mouth and the width of the nose.

The width of the nose and the distance between the nostrils.

The distance between the pupils and the distance between the eyebrows.

On a molecular level, the DNA molecule, which is the program for all life, is based on the golden mean which measures 34 angstroms long by 21 angstroms wide for each full cycle of its double helix spiral. 34 and 21 are numbers in the Fibonacci series and their ratio, 1.6190476 closely approximates phi, 1.6180339.

Dr. Stephen Marquardt has studied human beauty for years in his practice of oral and maxillofacial surgery. Marquardt performed cross-cultural surveys on beauty and found that all groups had the same perceptions of facial beauty. The more symmetric the face the more it is considered beautiful. He also analyzed the human face from ancient times to modern day. His research showed that beauty is not only related to phi, it can be defined for both genders and for all races, cultures, and eras, giving credence to the ancients who recognized the association in mathematics between beauty and truth.

Our consciousness resides at the center of our awareness in a magical infinity zone where inner meets outer, spirit meets matter, and the thoughts of our infinite inner reality interact with the infinity of "external" reality.

Every physical attribute of a human being is geometrically definable in three dimensions according to the cosmic laws of sacred geometry and the divine proportion.

The cosmic laws of sacred geometry also apply to the fourth dimension, time. The interplay of the dimensions of time and space through consciousness are made evident by applying geometric functions to the science of projective geometry.

These cosmic laws are self-apparent in geometric expression, and their truth is evident simply by examining them.

In the last two lines of John Keats's "Ode on a Grecian Urn", he stated:

"Beauty is truth, truth beauty,"-- that is all Ye know on earth, and all ye need to know.

This sentiment has its roots in prehistory and can be clearly seen in the enigmatic hieroglyphics and architecture of the ancient Egyptians, who saw no differences in science, art, and math.

For them, these diverse disciplines were all one and the same.

BEYOND THE OCTAVE

The number nine is not only three squared, it is the final single digit in our decimal system that precedes the next highest order, ten, symbolized by a one and a zero and it is the last digit preceding each progression of ten beyond that. Additionally, our physical bodies are bilateral, but we have ten toes and ten fingers with an opposable thumb; a physical advantage that ranks us at the top of the earth's animal hierarchy with the higher primates. Physiologically our digits are a prime external indicator of our place at the top of the evolutionary scale while internally, among other things, the development of our brain charts the path of the evolution of our consciousness into self-awareness; the capability that distinguishes us above all other life forms on the earth.

The term consciousness refers to common capabilities of humans and other animals, as well as to differentiate between them, designating uniquely human linguistic, rational, and abstract capabilities. Consciousness also includes a range of functions that esoteric traditions claim supersede rational and egoic forms of consciousness, representing the evolution of what is conceptualized as spirit, soul, mind, self, and transcendental human capabilities.

Shamanism, the oldest known form of spirituality in the world embraces all of these as well as all other forms of religious thought that followed in its footsteps. A basis for different forms of consciousness underlying shamanic phenomena is found in the major architectural and functional strata of the brain and their different information processes.

Although human consciousness is not specific to any particular function or system of the brain, different modalities of consciousness are associated with different systemic information-processing functions, integration of brain processes, and patterns of homeostasis. All of the major systems of the brain participate in complex human behavior, but specific systemic patterns of brain functioning are associated with distinct experiential states and modes of consciousness.

Recognition that consciousness is tied to the functioning of a biological system does not require reduction of consciousness solely to the functions of the biological system. A neurophenomenological approach illustrates that both epistemic constructs and physiological patterns of brain operation contribute to consciousness. The relationship of brain physiology to consciousness is illustrated through an examination of how the physical structures of the brain and their associated activities relate to patterns of consciousness.

The brain can be viewed as involving three anatomically distinct systems that are integrated to provide a range of behavioral, emotional, and informational functions. It is widely recognized that human's motor patterns, emotional states, and advanced cognitive and linguistic capabilities are primarily managed by brain systems that emerged sequentially in evolution. This triune brain model provides a framework for explicating the relationship between systemic brain activities and consciousness while relating to lower brain systems common with other animals and to unique aspects of the human brain.

The hierarchical tripartite triune brain is based on neuroanatomical, structural, and functional divisions that break down into three strata starting with the reptilian, followed by the paleomammalian, and neomammalian brains. The three formations have different anatomical structures that mediate different psychological and behavioral functions with their own forms of subjectivity, intelligence, time and space sense, memory capabilities, and motor functions. Although the three segments are integrated, they provide the basis for different capacities and represent a functional hierarchy of information-processing capabilities that provide the basis for distinct forms of consciousness.

The reptilian brain is composed of the upper spinal cord, portions of the mesencephalon (midbrain), the diencephalon (thalamus-hypothalamus), and the basal ganglia. The reptilian brain regulates organic functions such as metabolism, digestion, and respiration and it is responsible for wakefulness, attentional mechanisms, and the regulation and coordination of behavior.

The paleomammalian brain is based on evolutionary developments in the limbic system which provided distinctions between reptiles and mammals. This structure provides the basis for social behavior and nonverbal, emotional, and analogical information processing, and it functions as an emotional brain, mediating affect, sex, fighting/self defense, social relations, bonding and attachment, and the sense of self that provides the basis for beliefs, certainty, and convictions.

The neomammalian brain provides the basis for advanced symbolic processes, culture, language, logic, rational thought, analytical processes, and complex problem solving.

The reptilian brain provides the basic plots and actions of the body. The paleomammalian brain provides the emotional influences on thoughts and behavior, and the neomammalian brain uses enhanced symbolic capacities in elaborating on basic plots and emotions, integrating them with higher-level information processing.

The reptilian brain provides the organism with primary or simple awareness, which is adaptation to the environment through reflexes, conditioned responses, and habituation, as well as through instrumental learning.

The paleomammalian brain provides for qualities of consciousness enriched by self, other (society), and emotions, while the neomammalian brain encompassing the tertiary neocortical area and in particular the right hemisphere, and is involved in cross-integration and reorganization of perceptual modalities basic to symbolic cognition and self-awareness.

The neomammalian brain (neocortex and connecting thalamic structures) represents the most dramatic evolution of the brain. The expanded neocortex's functions are based on extensive connections with the visual, auditory, and somatic systems, indicating the primary orientation of the neocortex to the external world.

These three structures are also referred to as the three centers that we principally operate from, known from the top down as intellectual, emotional, and moving, that form a triad that relates to the every day functioning of our personality and they act as primary energizers that determine the way a person generally responds to stimuli.

A moving centered person will tend to be physically active and be fond of sports, travel, and action.

An emotionally centered person will tend to be more perceptive and will experience situations in terms of likes and dislikes.

An intellectually centered person will tend to be more verbal and will enjoy philosophy and thinking for its own sake.

Most people react from one of these centers, so when presented with any situation, their first immediate response will be either thought, feeling, or action, which represents the center they habitually rely on. If they react with thought they are intellectually centered, if they respond with feeling, they are emotionally centered, and if they respond with instantaneous action, they are moving centered.

People usually respond out of these three centers in a specific order. If they are intellectually centered they first react with thought, emotions will follow, then they act. If they are emotionally centered they feel first, act, then think about it later. Any combination of the three is possible as a habitual pattern based on their most developed center which comes first, and their least developed which comes last. The closer a person comes to operating simultaneously out of all three centers, the more integrated and effective they are.

When a person is paying attention (fully aware) they are more likely to feel, think, and act in unison. From this balanced point of power fears are neutralized and experience shifts to insight, relatedness, and beauty. Intentional awakening is fostered by the perception that one has not achieved one's potential.

In order to reach higher levels of awareness (Maslow's peak experience), three conditions are necessary; a powerful desire to know the truth, a willingness to be emotionally open to life, and a practiced ability to be balanced energetically. Intellectual, emotional, and moving centers form a triad which relates to the universal building blocks of love, energy, and truth, otherwise known as, love, power, and wisdom; a triad that manifests as inspiration, action, and expression.

A natural result of the evolution of the human brain is the fragmentation of consciousness, reflecting both the increasing modularity of consciousness and the diversification of self into more statuses. Shamanic traditions institutionalized procedures to overcome this fragmentation of consciousness by synchronizing this divergent human cognition through traditions using altered states of consciousness (ASC) to induce integrative brain processes. The shaman's use of external symbols and the relationships of the symbols to cultural psychodynamics engage transformative process through entraining neurocognitive structures, provoking a restructuring of the self at levels below conceptual and operational thought.

Shamanistic practices induce extraordinary experiences and healing by producing integrative relationships among brain systems and psychocultural beliefs. These experiences reflect the simultaneous elicitation and integration of normal modes of information processing and consciousness that do not ordinarily occur together. These ASC nonetheless involve normal integrative psychobiological processes elicited by many procedures.

A primary focus of the psychophysiological effects of shamanistic ASC is in the limbic system, or the paleomammalian brain. This brain area emerged in the evolution of mammals and provided a number of distinctive developments. Shamanistic healing is largely based on manipulation of processes and functions of the paleomammalian brain – self identity and social identity and their attachments, emotions, meanings, and references. Shamanistic ASC elicit processes of the paleomammalian brain and induce a systemic integration of information processing functions across the functional layers of the brain, producing limbic-cortical integration and interhemispheric synchronization.

Shamanistic healing practices achieve this integration by physically stimulating systematic brain wave discharge patterns that activate affects, memories, attachments, and other psychodynamic processes of the paleomammalian brain. This activation forces normally unconscious or preconscious primary information processing functions and outputs to be integrated into the operations of the frontal cortex. This integrates implicit understandings, socioemotional dynamics, repressed memories, unresolved conflicts, intuitions, and nonverbal – visual, mimetic, and presentational knowledge into self-conscious awareness.

The desire to alter consciousness is an innate human biologically based drive with adaptive significance. The ASC of shamanism are a manifestation of a fundamental homeostatic dynamic of the nervous system. These manifestations of consciousness involve a biologically based integrative mode of consciousness, replacing normal waking conditions – sympathetic dominance and desynchronized fast wave activity of the frontal cortex – with a parasympathetic dominant state characterized by high voltage, slow-wave electroencephalogram (EEG) activity originating in the circuits linking the brain stem and the hippocampal-septal area of the limbic system with the frontal cortex.

This high-voltage, slow wave EEG activity originates in the hippocampal-septal area and imposes a synchronous slow-wave pattern on the frontal lobes, producing interhemispheric synchronization and coherence, limbic-cortex integration, and integration across the neuraxis, resulting in a synthesis of behavior, emotion, and thought.

The parasympathetic state, slow-wave synchronization of the frontal cortex, and interhemispeheric integration reflect activation of basic aspects of brain operation related to sensory and physiological integration; mental and emotional integration; insight and transcendence; and interhemispheric integration.

A primary characteristic of integrative consciousness involves hierarchical integration of brain mechanisms, especially as manifested in limbic system driving of the frontal cortex through serotonergic induced integration across the neuraxis. This represents the integration of preconscious or unconscious functions and material into self conscious awareness.

There are four different biologically based modes of human consciousness – waking, sleep, dream, and integrative consciousness. These reflect the fundamental aspects of systemic functioning of the human organism that meet the following system functions and needs respectively: learning, adaptation, and survival needs (waking); recuperative functions, regeneration, and growth (deep sleep); memory integration and consolidation and psychosocial adaptation (dreaming); and psychodynamic growth and social and psychological integration (integrative).

The right hemisphere of the brain reflects a different symbolic form of representation in dreaming than that used in waking consciousness. The bizarreness of dreams reflects the imaginative and creative capacities of this presentational modality. Dreams appear bizarre and illogical from the point of view of waking consciousness because they involve a different system of information representation, processing, and consolidation. This visual-spatial system of symbolic presentation is normally inhibited by the dominance of left-hemisphere verbal representational systems; conditions that attenuate the left hemisphere's verbal representational systems allow expression of this presentational intelligence.

Meditation, rituals, hallucinogens and other shamanic practices can alter consciousness and physiological processes through a wide variety of mechanisms that induce retuning of the autonomic nervous system balance. This retuning tends to block the dominant hemisphere's functions and produces an integrative fusion with functions of the nondominant hemisphere. This structurally synchronized state tends to resolve internal conflicts and produce euphoric states. This synchronization depends on the elicitation of processes of lower brain structures that are associated with basic behavior, intentionality, and emotions.

These ASC evoke communicative responses from the paleomammalian brain that provide the basis for an expansion of consciousness by integrating information from the lower brain systems into operational activities of the frontal brain and by establishing synchrony with the frontal brain that permits symbolic reprogramming of the emotional dynamics and behavioral repertoires of lower brain centers.

When the triune brain works in unison and the individual operates simultaneously out of all three centers, the more integrated and effective they are because they are fully aware. The instinctual, emotional, and intellectual centers will feel, think, and act simultaneously from a balanced point of power where fears are neutralized and experience shifts to insight, relatedness, and beauty.

When there is a homeostatic dynamic of the nervous system a biologically based integrative mode of consciousness comes into play replacing normal waking conditions – sympathetic dominance and desynchronized fast wave activity of the frontal cortex with a parasympathetic dominant state.

In essence, the slow-wave synchronization of the frontal cortex is the energy that comes from transcending the male and female polarities, creating a triad that focuses on the energy manifest between them as opposed to that of the extremes.

Three brains from the top down working in unison to produce a fully aware state of insight, relatedness, and beauty combined with the right "female" brain and the left "male" brain working in synchronization and coherence, synthesizing behavior, emotion, and thought to produce a slow-wave synchronization of the third frontal cortex indicate sensory and physiological integration; mental and emotional integration; resulting in insight and transcendence.

This fully turned on 3 X 3 brain brings a radical shift in

consciousness that could produce a shift from our present fourth dimensional existence that perceives a three dimensional world, to a possible fifth dimension where we perceive the fourth dimension, transcending time and duality. A transcendence from 2^2, 2 X 2, the model for three dimensional existence to the next logical progression of 3^2, 3 X 3, the number 9 may very well be the new model for the fifth dimension which is often referred to as the second coming of Christ consciousness or the return of Quetzalcoatl.

Aside from the continuing breakthroughs in quantum physics that prove that material reality is in fact consciousness, there can be no doubt that profound changes are upon us. Global warming is a fact, as is a shift in the magnetic poles of our planet, and an upward shift in the internal frequency of our planet.

The earth's frequency was previously thought to be constant. When NASA started measuring it, it was 7.8 hertz. It has been measured as high as 14 and it is speeding up. At the same time the field strength of the earth's gravity is dropping at an alarming rate. In the last few years magnetic north has been moving rapidly, and the inner core of the earth has displaced itself from the angle of rotation of the earth's crust. The sun's own magnetic north and south is no longer detectable as of 1995 and solar flares and proton storms are off the scale. On December 22, 2012 the sun was in alignment with the galactic equator of the Milky Way Galaxy. This occurs every 25,800 years and was predicted by the Mayans. This is also the date of the birth of Venus, which represents the feminine, the right brain intuitive energy that has been suppressed for far too long.

Energetically all of these phenomena represent an electromagnetic shift upward. The results of what occurs from an increase in frequency were proven in Cymatics, the study of wave phenomena, a science pioneered by Swiss medical doctor and natural scientist, Hans Jenny (1904-1972). Jenny conducted experiments animating inert powders, pastes, and liquids into life-like flowing forms that mirrored patterns found throughout nature, art, and architecture. These patterns were created using simple sine wave vibrations using pure tones within the audible range so observers could see a physical representation of vibration, or how sound manifests into form through the medium of various materials.

Among other things, Cymatics shows that when vibrational patterns were produced in series and compared, the same formal pattern recurred at increasing frequencies. The number of constituent elements also increased at the higher frequencies. At a particular frequency a specific matrix pattern forms, then with an increase in frequency the pattern dissolves into chaos before reforming into a more complex pattern at a higher frequency.

In other words chaos precedes reformation from a lower order into a more complex, higher order. The old structure has to break down in order for the new more complex one to form. When we are born into this world we go from amniotic bliss through the chaos and violence of the birth process until we are born anew into a whole new paradigm of being.

It has become clear that numerous unprecedented changes are occurring within and around us and we are feeling our subjective experience of time moving faster and faster because our consciousness is quickening in preparation for what very well could be an upcoming dimensional shift. If we are aware enough to be in harmony with the natural unfolding cosmic laws of oneness, reciprocity, and balance, and we are in harmony and alignment within ourselves, living in full integrity and unity with all that is, we may ride the wave and flow forward with the ongoing shift to the next higher dimension along with our mother earth, and we just might become fully conscious co-creators of our reality.

PORTAL TO THE INFINITE

Expanding and contracting geometric progressions can manifest in endless permutations through every day visible expressions and throughout microcosmic quantum realms, and the deeper we delve into these puzzling realities the more bizarre and unpredictable they become. We live at the center of a Great Mystery and in spite of our advanced technologies we are no closer to the truth, in fact as we have seen, our sophisticated technologies driven by our divide and conquer mentality have only succeeded in isolating us from the natural world even more.

Moving from esoteric concerns into the realm of the biological, we fear what we can't comprehend and act like little children who are afraid of the dark until we become en*light*ened, proving and reinforcing the fact that fear is contraction and love is expansion.

Faced with the Great Mystery of our existence we can "bury our heads in the sand" and continue losing ourselves and the world we live in through the mirrors of our narcissistic cell phone and internet consumer culture or in many other cultural distractions that we have created with the transitory "magic" of our technology, reinforcing our distance from the natural world, or we can face the grand mystery of something much bigger than we are.

If we look deep within ourselves and see the above and below of our inner and outer worlds and realize that we have the unique position of straddling them both, we can realize the perfect reflection of holographic truth that we exist within.

Regardless of the path we might take, if we follow the unfolding self-evident maps, where might they take us?

What happens when our short lived sojourn here on the planet earth ends?

We can only speculate what death brings in our release from three dimensional reality and we can push the limits of our consciousness through exploratory altered states the way shamans have since time immemorial, cracking open inner space and storming heaven to the best of our abilities, but regardless of what we may learn and experience, what happens after we die is still a mystery that will only be revealed when we cross that threshold - alone.

No matter the source, we owe it to ourselves to consider any possibilities that might present themselves, and if they have any ring of truth, there is no harm in acknowledging what might resonate with us at the core of our being.

Anything is possible.

In this spirit, a gifted teacher, sound healer, psychotherapist, and singer named Tom Kenyon channels what he calls the Hathors, who say they are a group of interdimensional, intergalactic beings who were connected in ancient Egypt through the Temples of the Goddess Hathor as well as several other prehistoric cultures. Kenyon says that he was "contacted" by them during meditation in the late 1980's when they began instructing him in the vibratory nature of the cosmos, the use of sacred geometry as a means to stimulate brain performance, and in the use of sound to activate psycho-spiritual experiences.

Among the many messages that the Hathors have given, the one transcribed below resonates with and carries the most relevance in relation to what has been written in this book, particularly in regard to death and speculation about what might occur in passing from the here and now of the physical plane into the Great Mystery that awaits us all.

"The nexus of our message is one of personal empowerment and freedom, so we caution you as you enter into the fifth and higher dimensional realities to avoid alien implanted delusions that there are other beings you should bow down to. Honor them if they are honorable, yes. Bow down to anyone? Never!

"At the completion of your biological death, from our experience and perspective, you will be confronted with three portals. The first is a tunnel of light. The second is a portal opened through the energetics of a guru or

savior. And the third is a portal, or tunnel, that leads into darkness.

The tunnel of light is generated from the pranic tube that runs through the center of your body, which runs from your perineum to your crown, and it is a tunnel-like or tube-like channel. At the moment of death, your consciousness moves upward through this tunnel that opens into another dimension of consciousness through your crown chakra.

On the other side of this tunnel is a bright light, and you may find yourself sensing that you are on a bridge crossing over a stream or a river. On the other side of the bridge will be those persons of your previous life, the lifetime you have just ended. You may sense those who have died before you, including pets you have had, because the animal spirits also dwell in this realm. If there are incomplete relationships or issues still to be resolved with these persons or beings, you may feel a yearning to enter this light, and by doing so you re-enter the wheel of birth and death, and you will reincarnate— most likely on Earth.

The second portal is created by the personal will of a guru or savior. Entering this portal will lead you into the vibratory field of the guru or savior that you have a deep personal connection to. And for those of you on this path, entering this dimension of consciousness will be the completion of a profound desire to be with this being. Our caution here is that you will be entering a realm defined not only by the evolutionary attainment of your guru or savior but also by his or her limitations.

The third portal opens into darkness. And entering this portal leads you into the Void, the creatrix from which all things arise. If you choose this portal and have prepared yourself to deal with this level of freedom you will be freed to explore other dimensions of this cosmos and beyond, meaning states of being that transcend all physical phenomena. In this realm of existence you can become an explorer of other realities as you so choose."

Is there any truth in these enigmatic words?

Only time will tell and we will all discover the answers when we find ourselves at the portal that leads us out of the three dimensional world that we have been living in and we once more get to see how the mystery unfolds.

Recommended Reading

Abrams, David, *The Spell Of The Sensuous: Perception And Language In a More-Than -Human World*, (New York: Random House, 1996)

Calleman, Carl J., *Solving the Greatest Mystery of Our Time: The Mayan Calendar*, (Coral Springs: Garev, 2001)

Campbell, Joseph, *The Hero With A Thousand Faces*, (Novato: New World Library)

Doreal, Dr. M., *The Emerald Tablets of Thoth The Atlantean.* (Nashville: Source Books, 2002)

Eliade, Mircea, *Shamanism, Archaic Techniques of Ecstasy*, (Princeton: University Press, 2004)

Friedman, Robert L., *The Healing Power of the Drum*, (Philadelphia: White Cliffs Media Co, 2000)

Haule, John R., *Taking Direction from the Spirit in Shamanism and Psychotherapy*, (Shamanic Applications Review 1997)

Havelock, Eric A., *The Muse Learns to Write*, (New Haven: Yale University Press, 1988)

Jenny, Hans, *Cymatics: A Study of Wave Phenomena and Vibration*, (Newmarket: MACROmedia, 2001)

Jung, Carl, *The Portable Jung*, (New York: Penguin, 1976)

Jung, Carl, *The Psychology of the Transference*, (Princeton: Princeton University Press, 1959)

Jung, Carl, *The Undiscovered Self*, (New York: Signet Books, 2006)

Jung, Carl, *Symbols of Transformation*, (New York: Pantheon, 1956)

Kenyon, Tom, *The Hathor Material: Messages From an Ascended Civilization*, (Baltimore: Orb Communications, 2012)

Lawlor, Robert, *Sacred Geometry: Philosophy & Practice*, (London: Thames & Hudson, 1982)

MacLean, P., *The Triune Concept of Brain and Behavior*,   (Toronto: University of Toronto Press, 1973)

MacLean, P., *The Triune Brain in Evolution*, (New York: Plenum Press, 1990)
McKee, Robert, *Story*, (New York: Regan Books, 1997)

McKenna, Terence, *Food of the Gods*, (New York: Bantam Books, 1992)

McNeley, James K., *Holy Wind in Navajo Philosophy*, (Tucson: University of Arizona Press, 1981)

Merkur, Dan, *Becoming Half Hidden: Shamanism and Initiation Among the Inuit*, (New York: Garland Publishing, 1992)

Merleau-Ponty, Maurice, *Phenomenology of Perception*, (London: Routledge & Kegan Paul, 1962)

Ouspensky, Pyotr D., *In Search of the Miraculous*. (San Diego: Harcourt Brace, 1949)

Pallamary, Matthew, J., *Spirit Matters*, (San Diego: Mystic Ink Publishing, 2007)

Pallamary, Matthew, J., Mayberry, Paul, *The Infinity Zone*, (San Diego: Mystic Ink Publishing, 2012)

Pallamary, Matthew, J., *Phantastic Fiction*, (San Diego: Mystic Ink Publishing, 2015)

Schwaller de Lubicz, R. A., *The Temple in Man*, (Rochester: Inner Traditions, 1981)

Schwaller de Lubicz, R. A., *The Temple of Man*, (Rochester: Inner Traditions, 1998)

Sheldrake, Rupert, Morphic Resonance: The Nature of Formative Causation, (Rochester: Park Street Press, 2009)

Steiner, Rudolph, *The Fourth Dimension: Sacred Geometry, Alchemy, and Mathematics*, (Great Barrington: Anthroposophic Press, 2001)

Stevens, José, *Earth to Tao*, (Santa Fe: Bear and Company, 1994)

Talbot, Michael, *The Holographic Universe*, (New York: Harper Perennial, 2011)

Vogler, Christopher, *The Writer's Journey: Mythic Structure For Writers*, (Studio City: Michael Wiese Productions, 2007)

Winkelman, Michael, *Shamanism: The Neural Ecology of Consciousness and Healing*, (Westport: Bergin & Garvey, 2000)

ABOUT THE AUTHOR

Matthew J. Pallamary's works have been translated into Spanish, Portuguese, Italian, Norwegian, French, and German. His historical novel of first contact between shamans and Jesuits in 18th century South America, titled, *Land Without Evil* received rave reviews along with a San Diego Book Award for mainstream fiction. It was also adapted into a full-length stage and sky show, co-written with Agent Red, directed by Agent Red, and performed by Sky Candy, an Austin Texas aerial group. The making of the show was the subject of a PBS series, Arts in Context episode, which garnered an EMMY nomination.

His nonfiction book, *The Infinity Zone: A Transcendent Approach to Peak Performance* is a collaboration with professional tennis coach Paul Mayberry that offers a fascinating exploration of the phenomenon that occurs at the nexus of perfect form and motion. *The Infinity Zone* took 1st place in the International Book Awards, New Age category and was a finalist in the San Diego Book Awards.

His first book, a short story collection titled *The Small Dark Room Of The Soul* was mentioned in The Year's Best Horror and Fantasy and received praise from Ray Bradbury.

His second collection, *A Short Walk to the Other Side* was an Award Winning Finalist in the International Book Awards, an Award Winning Finalist in the USA Best Book Awards, and an Award Winning Finalist in the San Diego Book Awards.

DreamLand a novel about computer generated dreaming, written with legendary DJ Ken Reeth won first place in the Independent e-Book Award in the Horror/Thriller category and was an Award

Winning Finalist in the San Diego Book Awards.

It's sequel, *n0thing* is titled after the main character, who in the real world is his nephew, an international Counter-Strike gaming champion. After winning what amounts to the Super Bowl of gaming, n0thing and his winning teammates, are recruited as a literal "dream team" whose mission is to go into the nightmares of battle scarred veterans and rescue them from their traumatic memories while becoming ambassadors for a gaming platform that exceeds virtual reality with an experience that pushes the boundaries of reality itself.

Eye of the Predator was an Award Winning Finalist in the Visionary Fiction category of the International Book Awards. *Eye of the Predator* is a supernatural thriller about a zoologist who discovers that he can go into the minds of animals.

CyberChrist was an Award Winning Finalist in the Thriller/Adventure category of the International Book Awards. *CyberChrist* is the story of a prize winning journalist who receives an email from a man who claims to have discovered immortality by turning off the aging gene in a 15 year old boy with an aging disorder. The forwarded email becomes the basis for an online church built around the boy, calling him CyberChrist.

Phantastic Fiction - A Shamanic Approach to Story took first place in the International Book Awards Writing/Publishing category. *Phantastic Fiction* is Matt's guide to dramatic writing that grew out of his popular Phantastic Fiction Workshop.

Night Whispers was an Award Winning Finalist in the Horror category of the International Book Awards. Set in the Boston neighborhood of Dorchester, *Night Whispers* is the story of Nick Powers, who loses consciousness after crashing in a stolen car and comes to hearing whispering voices in his mind. When he sees a homeless man arguing with himself, Nick realizes that the whispers in his head are the other side of the argument.

His memoir *Spirit Matters* detailing his journeys to Peru, working with shamanic plant medicines took first place in the San Diego Book Awards Spiritual Book Category, and was an Award-Winning Finalist in the autobiography/memoir category of the National Best Book Awards. *Spirit Matters* is also available as an audio book.

Matt has also produced and directed ***The Santa Barbara Writers Conference Scrapbook*** documentary film and co-wrote the book of the same title in collaboration with Y. Armando Nieto, and conference founder Mary Conrad.

His work has appeared in Oui, New Dimensions, The Iconoclast, Starbright, Infinity, Passport, The Short Story Digest, Redcat, The San Diego Writer's Monthly, Connotations, Phantasm, Essentially You, The Haven Journal, The Montecito Journal, and many others. His fiction has been featured in The San Diego Union Tribune which he has also reviewed books for, and his work has been heard on KPBS-FM in San Diego, KUCI FM in Irvine, television Channel Three in Santa Barbara, and The Susan Cameron Block Show in Vancouver. He has been a guest on the following nationally syndicated talk shows; Paul Rodriguez, In The Light with Michelle Whitedove, Susun Weed, Medicine Woman, Inner Journey with Greg Friedman, and Environmental Directions Radio series. Matt has appeared on the following television shows; Bridging Heaven and Earth, Elyssa's Raw and Wild Food Show, Things That Matter, Literary Gumbo, Indie Authors TV, and ECONEWS. He has also been a frequent guest on numerous podcasts, among them, The Psychedelic Salon, Black Light in the Attic, Third Eye Drops, C-Realm, and others.

Matt received the Man of the Year Award from San Diego Writer's Monthly Magazine and has taught a fiction workshop at the Southern California Writers' Conference in San Diego, Palm Springs, and Los Angeles, and at the Santa Barbara Writers' Conference for twenty five years. He has lectured at the Greater Los Angeles Writer's Conference, the Getting It Write conference in Oregon, the Saddleback Writers' Conference, the Rio Grande Writers' Seminar, the National Council of Teachers of English, The San Diego Writer's and Editor's Guild, The San Diego Book Publicists, The Pacific Institute for Professional Writing, The 805 Writers Conference, and he has been a panelist at the World Fantasy Convention, Con-Dor, and Coppercon. He is presently Editor in Chief of Mystic Ink Publishing.

He has been teaching at the Santa Barbara Writers Conference, the Southern California Writers Conference, and many other venues for the past twenty five years and frequently visits the mountains, deserts, and jungles of North, Central, and South America pursuing his studies of shamanism.

WWW.MATTPALLAMARY.COM

BOOKS BY MATTHEW J. PALLAMARY

THE SMALL DARK ROOM OF THE SOUL

LAND WITHOUT EVIL

SPIRIT MATTERS

DREAMLAND (WITH KEN REETH)

THE INFINITY ZONE (WITH PAUL MAYBERRY)

A SHORT WALK TO THE OTHER SIDE

CYBERCHRIST

EYE OF THE PREDATOR

PHANTASTIC FICTION

NIGHT WHISPERS

THE SANTA BARABARA WRITERS CONFERENCE SCRAPBOOK
(WITH MARY CONRAD & Y. ARMANDO NIETO)

n0THING

84382146R00129

Made in the USA
Columbia, SC
28 December 2017